Praise for *The Maste*

D0558143

"The Master Keys of Healing *is writte*
Alan Cohen at his very best, a marvelous ~~book. I think it should be called,~~
"The Complete Guide to Spiritual and Bodily Healing." *It is a must-*
read for everyone, full of wisdom and practical advice. Alan reminds
us so clearly and eloquently that wellness is our natural state, and he
guides us back to our wholeness. This book is so appropriate at this time
when the world is gripped by fear and trepidation. I cannot sing enough
praises about this fantastic book! I will be re-reading it many times."

— Dr. Catherine O'Connell, Family Physician,
Bachelor of Medicine, Bachelor of Surgery,
Diploma in Child Health, Diploma of the Royal College
of Obstetricians and Gynecologists, Member of the
Royal College of General Practice, with Distinction.

"The Master Keys of Healing *is one of the most impactful and*
important books I have read in decades. As a busy clinician who has
worked with thousands of clients and many celebrities, I can say with
complete conviction that this book should be the required textbook for
anyone going through any healing journey. It is whole and holy in the
truest sense, a timeless map of an ancient journey. As I read, I would
internally reference study after scientific study. It is scientifically valid.
As someone who also personally healed from two years of a chronic
illness, it is a complete reflection of the internal alchemy of true healing.
I could not put this book down. Almost every sentence is highlighted.
This book is a Way Maker and a sacred Compass and I recommend it
wholeheartedly with compelling love."

— Dr. Matt Lyon, Doctor of Chiropractic,
Master's in Acupuncture and Oriental Medicine,
Chinese Herbal Medicine, and Functional Medicine

"Alan Cohen is an author who skillfully heals others with his soothing
wisdom. After 40 years of serving as a doctor, I am still amazed by the
various keys of healing available. In this most helpful book, Alan shares
many examples of these keys and why healing is possible, available, and
above all dependent on how we choose between love and fear. In my busy
clinic, hardly a day passes where I do not apply what I learned from this
book—which should be read for information, inspiration, and application."

— Dr. Peter Nieman, FRCP FAAP, President
of the Alberta Chapter of the American Academy
of Pediatrics, holistic health coach, marathon runner,
and author of *Moving Forward*

"I love this book, as I have loved all of Alan's books! Alan's great stories make the ideas very concrete and clear. This book would make a great textbook for a course in healing or wellness offered at a university—but it is also a great book for one's own self-study of healing and wellness for people who want to heal themselves and/or stay well! This is a book I believe everyone should read, especially at this time when fear is so rampant on the planet! Our whole country is suffering from fear of epidemics, cancer, heart disease, drug addiction, depression, and suicide. Alan makes it clear that the goal of healing the planet needs to begin with oneself, and "owning" one's own divinity. We can experience our lives here as living in heaven, or hell. I'm choosing heaven for myself, and for all of us!"*

— Dr. Frances Delahanty, Ph.D., emeritus Professor, Pace University, Pleasantville, NY, Certified New York State Psychologist, Certified Holistic Life Coach

"Filled with many pearls of wisdom, this book is a must for those seeking healing and for those in the healing profession. As a primary care physician for over forty years, I have noticed the patients who are ultimately healed are those who actively collaborate with me in the healing process. Alan reminds us of our own ability to heal ourselves and also reminds the healer of their part in the shared process."

— Dr. Teresa Reid, MD, FAAP, previous Associate Professor of Pediatrics, University of Minnesota School of Medicine, Certified Holistic Life Coach

"With stories that will open your mind and touch your heart, Alan Cohen shares The Master Keys of Healing with his usual deep insight, gentle humor, and profound compassion. Showing us how to move past our feelings of unworthiness or fear, Alan's words will empower those who seek to be healers and comfort those in need of healing. In these wounded and confusing times, The Master Keys of Healing is a prescription that will make us all feel better. I'll be using many of his valuable keys in my own practice and am grateful to Mr. Cohen for making me a better healer."

— Dr. Michael Klaper, M.D., Primary Care Physician, Director, Moving Medicine Forward Initiative, author of *Vegan Nutrition: Pure and Simple*

Also by Alan Cohen

Are You as Happy as Your Dog?

A Course in Miracles Made Easy

Dare to Be Yourself

A Deep Breath of Life

A Daily Dose of Sanity

Don't Get Lucky, Get Smart

The Dragon Doesn't Live Here Anymore

Enough Already

The Grace Factor

Handle with Prayer

Happily Even After

Have You Hugged a Monster Today?

I Had It All the Time

How Good Can It Get?

Joy Is My Compass

Lifestyles of the Rich in Spirit

Linden's Last Life

Looking In for Number One

My Father's Voice

The Peace That You Seek

Relax into Wealth

Rising in Love

Setting the Seen

Spirit Means Business

The Tao Made Easy

Why Your Life Sucks and What You Can Do about It

Wisdom of the Heart

The
MASTER
KEYS
of
HEALING

The MASTER KEYS *of* HEALING

CREATING DYNAMIC WELL-BEING FROM THE INSIDE OUT

ALAN COHEN

ISBN: 978-0-910367-09-7

Ebook ISBN:- 978-0-910367-07-3

Printed in the United States of America

For Hilda and Bruno,
whose pure intention to heal and serve
have blessed my life
and millions more

CONTENTS

INTRODUCTION

At a motivational conference I met a fellow who had been diagnosed with a rare debilitating disease. For seven years Stephen consulted with over a hundred doctors, submitted to endless tests, ingested more than a hundred prescription pills daily, and tried a wide range of treatments, none of which helped. He kept losing weight until he was down to 120 pounds. A final experiment with a risky drug failed. His doctor told him, "You will soon die."

At that moment Stephen got fed up with depending on doctors to save him, and instead he turned within. He affirmed over and over and over again, "I am healed." After six weeks of intensive introspection and affirmation, Stephen began to feel better and his symptoms started to disappear. He gained weight and gradually eliminated his medications. Eventually he was restored to perfect health and he felt fantastic. Now Stephen looks radiant, lives a full life, works from home, and spends many valued hours a day with his wife and three children. He is a walking miracle.

Is Stephen an exception to the laws of health, or is he a demonstration that healing is available to all of us, often in ways other than we have traditionally expected? Do we really need to struggle to feel good, pay exorbitant sums of money, and depend on external sources to maintain or restore our well-being? Can healing be simpler, easier, more direct, and less costly than we have been told?

In many classic adventures, the hero is given a special instruction manual to escape from trouble and find a way home. Dorothy in *The Wizard of Oz*, flung worlds away from her farmhouse by a tornado, meets Good Witch Glinda, who directs her to the yellow brick road leading to the wizard who can get her back to Kansas. Indiana Jones opens his mailbox to find a mysterious journal of tattered yellow pages, a map to the Holy Grail. In *Illusions*, barnstormer Richard Bach meets an incognito spiritual master who bestows upon him the tiny wisdom-packed *Messiah's Handbook*. The nonfiction classic *Be Here Now* chronicles Ram Dass's legendary journey to India, where a mystic takes him on a wild ride through the Himalayas and introduces him to the guru who transforms his life.

The book you are holding contains all the wisdom you will ever need to heal yourself and others. It is a precise roadmap to the well-being you seek. If you apply the truths revealed in the pages that follow, your life will change and you will uplift others. I did not invent these principles and they are not new. They are emblazoned into the fabric of the universe. I have simply applied natural laws and proven that they work. Because they are rock solid, they will work for you too.

The master keys of healing are not hidden, secret, or esoteric. They but *seem* mysterious because most people are distracted, looking every place but where they are. These principles have been shouted from the rooftops by every great seer, sage, and spiritual master since the first human fell ill. Yet only those who are open to receive higher truth can reap its rewards. If you are reading these words, you are ready. You may be tempted to put them aside because they seem too simple or challenge your long-standing beliefs, but you will come back to this book or one like it when you are ripe. You are not free to establish the curriculum for healing. You simply elect when you want to take it.

The world teaches us that we will find healing in endless places other than where it lives. Go to this doctor, take this pill, adopt this diet, join this group. All such efforts can certainly help; many qualified practitioners and methods can bring us closer to our goal. I am not suggesting that you avoid doctors or medical treatments, which serve as channels for wellness. I *am* suggesting that you pierce to the source from which all healing springs. You do not need to go out for your remedy. You need to go in. If you are tired of seeking help from external agents and receiving no relief or temporary relief, becoming more confused and frustrated, you may ask, "Where does it all end?"

It ends here. Now. With you. At this moment you have access to all the well-being you could ever need. No intermediary is required. No elixirs to buy, no exotic place to travel to, nothing to do but allow the power within you to heal you. The purpose of this book is to help you find genuine, lasting, soul-satisfying wellness of body, mind, and spirit, and remove you from the pool of misery that tragically characterizes humanity. I want you to recognize your absolute, inherent, God-given right to feel good and have your body function at optimal efficiency. I want you to enjoy intimate, loving, rewarding, enduring relationships. I want you to live in an abundant universe that provides for all of your material needs. I want you to break free of struggle and dwell in grace.

It is my intention in the pages that follow to advance the world toward the end of disease. While that mission may sound audacious, consider how quickly many long-standing limiting beliefs have fallen. The time between the Wright Brothers' first airplane flight and the moon landing was but

65 years—the tiniest flick in the grand march of evolution. If in 1904 someone suggested that a man would walk on the moon in less than one lifetime, that person would have been branded insane. Beware what you accept as fact and what you write off as fantasy; the two are often reversed.

We are about to step into territory that belongs now only to possibility, yet will become reality. We will mobilize the change of mind that restores your body and your life. No greater journey has ever been taken, and ultimately no other journey exists. The sails are hoisted and the wind is at our back. Let us begin.

A NEW WAY
of
SEEING

THE TRUTH ABOUT YOU

The life that I have lived was no more
than a mask covering the real me.
What has happened was not to kill me but to reveal me.

—E'YEN A. GARDNER

In my college library I passed an exhibit displaying the chemical remains of a person who had died; the tiny pile of powder was small enough to fit in the palm of a hand. Next to the mound sat a printed legend detailing the elements the mound contained, like carbon, potassium, and phosphorus. The legend also estimated the number of times this person's heart had beat, his lungs had breathed, and he had made love. This capsule story put a human life in stunning perspective. At a time in my life when pulsing, breathing, and lovemaking were way up on the list of desirable activities, I found the lesson sobering.

I began to consider the questions we all must eventually address: Is there more to me than my body? Do I have a life more substantial than my physical experience? Am I limited by what my body can or cannot do? Am I defined by my personality, childhood traumas, gender, weight, or astrological sign? Do I have a self greater than my self-concept? Will a part of me outlive my earthly casing? Can I heal my life by changing who I think I am? Who am I really?

Identity by Choice

Emil Ratalband, a 69-year-old Dutch man, recently petitioned a court to allow him to change his legal age to 49. He argued that he feels 20 years younger, and medical tests indicate his physical age to be equivalent to a man in his forties. Courts are now allowing transgender individuals to change their legal gender, so why not allow someone to change their legal age? At the time of this writing, Ratalband's case is being considered by Dutch legal authorities. Regardless the result, the man raises some important questions about defining ourselves by the age of our body or by any other physical aspect. The more we identify with a number of years, the more we take on the attributes commonly associated with that number. So if you state a lower age, the age that you feel, on a job application or dating website, are you really lying, or are you telling a deeper truth? Would it not be a bigger lie to claim an age that is older than you feel, act, and physically test to be? I believe that Mr. Ratalband is on the right track, at least in principle; perhaps he will serve as a pioneer for many of us to break free of cultural conditioning that pigeonholes human beings according to the number of trips we have made around the sun.

Within you lives a person far grander than the identities you have adopted. Now the time has come for you to release your untapped greatness. My client Mandy is a very shy young woman. She dresses plainly, wears no makeup, does not date, and withdraws from groups of people. She is a classic introvert. A few years ago Mandy took up puppeteering and grew so excited about the craft that she built an elaborate puppet theater and developed ingenious, colorful puppets and clever shows. Now Mandy regularly presents at schools and community events. When I went to see Mandy's show, I was floored. The program was lively, dramatic, funny, and highly entertaining. The puppets joked, sang, and argued. Mandy's puppets are everything she is not in her normal life. All of her repressed creativity and self-expression come forth through her puppets. As a result, she brings delight to others and enjoys a substantial livelihood. Who is Mandy really? Is she the shy introvert, or is she the flamboyant entertainer? We might say that she is both. Yet when she allows the brighter one to come forth, she begets results that match it.

When many years ago I met the esteemed spiritual guide Ram Dass, I was enamored with him as a teacher. His profound lessons transformed my life; to me he was a prophet of God. Starry-eyed, I followed Ram Dass around, learned everything I could from him, and strove to emulate him. Though he did not encourage it, I was a groupie.

Over decades I developed my own teaching practice and gained confidence in myself and my work. As destiny would have it, Ram Dass moved to a house just a few miles from where I lived on Maui. We became friends and I began to spend quality time with the man I most respected.

Then Ram Dass invited me to co-present a program with him. After the thrill and honor of the invitation, anxiety set in. Would I hold my own with him? Would my adoration for this mentor leak through and undermine my presentation? Would I get nervous and say or do something stupid? Suddenly I reverted to the starry-eyed groupie I had been thirty years earlier.

After wrestling with my upcoming role, I realized I was being called to choose between two distinctly different identities: a young adoring fan, or a mature spiritual teacher. I could not be both—I had to be one or the other. After much introspection, I decided to be the person I had become rather than one I had been. Being a confident leader felt far more empowering than being a needy follower. I went on to present from that stronger identity, and the program went extremely well. Ram Dass has since invited me to co-present with him numerous times, and all of the events have been successful and fun.

At every moment you, too, are choosing the identity you will claim, which determines the results you beget. There is a powerful link between who you believe you are, how you feel, and the success you achieve. News stories recount mothers who lift heavy dressers that fell on their babies, a feat of strength impossible under normal circumstances; football players who complete a game with a broken arm or leg; and people who rise from their deathbed when inspired with a reason to live. Psychology stimulates biology. Mind directs matter. When you find the inner healthy person, the healthy outer person follows.

In stating his case to change his legal age, Emil Ratalband declared, "I am a young god." His declaration applies equally to you and me. We are all ageless, vital expressions of God, no matter our physical experience. To claim you are a god is not arrogant; it represents extreme humility to acknowledge you are created in the image and likeness of God. Jesus, quoting scripture, asked the people, "Have you not been told that you are gods?" Jesus was crucified for claiming that he was the son of God. If you claim the same, you may also get pushback from people steeped in smallness. But the fact remains that the spark of God lives within you, as you. That brilliant flame has no age and it cannot be sick or die. When you identify with the God in you rather than your frail mortal coil, you live the destiny for which you were born.

J.D. Salinger stated, "The mark of the immature man is that he wants to die nobly for a cause, while the mark of the mature man is that he wants to live humbly for one." Ultimately the only cause we live for is to remember and help each other remember that our deepest, truest nature is divine. We are not broken, but whole; not sinful, but innocent; not abandoned, but beloved. We are far, far more than little piles of chemicals.

MASTER KEYS *of* THIS CHAPTER

1. There is far more to you than the elements of your body or the physical world. Your spiritual nature transcends anything the five senses perceive.

2. You are not defined or limited by your physical age. Your mental, emotional, and spiritual experience more accurately represents the real you.

3. While you may present a certain image to the world, the inner you is far more important.

4. You are not arrogant to claim that you are an expression of God. It is more arrogant to claim that you are not an expression of God. All that God is, you are.

5. Any definition of yourself as broken, lacking, or limited is erroneous. At all times you are whole, abundant, and unlimited.

THE PENTHOUSE
AND THE SLUMS

*Both abundance and lack exist simultaneously
in our lives, as parallel realities.*

*It is always our conscious choice which
secret garden we will tend.*

—SARAH BAN BREATHNACH

In the intriguing movie *Passion of Mind,* Demi Moore plays a woman who is living a double life. In one reality she is Marty, a savvy career woman cutting book deals in Manhattan. In her other life she is Marie, a widowed mother of two small children, nursing her broken heart in a charming chateau in the French countryside. When Marty goes to sleep in New York, she finds herself in France, and when Marie closes her eyes on her French day, she carries on with her American life. Each life is equally real when she is in it, and they both become more involved and intense until she nearly goes crazy trying to figure out who she really is. Eventually she decides that one life is a dream and she relinquishes it in favor of the other's reality.

While the notion of simultaneous alternative realities is often presented as fiction, there is far more truth to it than most people realize. It is, in fact, a fundamental key to healing. In this chapter we will explore your power to achieve healing or any form of success by tapping into the reality in which your goal is already so.

Even in the physical world, strikingly different realities exist side by side. I saw a photograph of a luxury high-rise condominium complex in India. The gleaming tower boasted a swimming pool on the deck of each unit, stacked upon each other and fanned at an angle like cards at a casino. At the base of the tower stood two tennis courts and a large community swimming pool amid lush landscaping. Only the ultra-wealthy could afford such extravagant digs. On the other side of a fence was the bleakest of slums, small dilapidated hovels crowded together in a hodgepodge mess, bordered by crooked, cracked muddy streets, not one green living plant growing in its midst. The contrast between the two lifestyles was staggering.

Just as those two entirely discontinuous realities stand side by side, an infinite number of realities co-exist in the same universe. Jesus said, "In my Father's house there are many mansions," meaning that there are as many realms of consciousness as a mind can imagine—and far more. The manifest universe contains all things wonderful and all things horrible; lavish riches and abysmal poverty; heavenly dreams and hellish nightmares. Illness represents one distinct reality, and vibrant health another. At every moment we are choosing which realm we will dwell in.

This Can't Be It

The world we have been taught is so substantial, is not. It is more amorphous than solid; more myth than fact; more the Emperor's fictitious wardrobe than his unfeathered underwear. What appears to be true is often the inverse of truth, a photographic negative in which black seems white and white seems black. The world that passes before us daily is inconsistent, untrustworthy, and fundamentally insane. *A Course in Miracles* tells us, "Not one thing the world believes is true."

You have been taught that if you can just make the grade in the real world, you will be happy. Yet many who rise to the heights of that *apparently* real world are miserable. If beauty, talent, fame, wealth, and power make us happy, why would a good-hearted, world-beloved talent like Robin Williams tragically take his own life? Why would a lovely A-list actress who earned millions of dollars for her starring roles, be arrested for petty shoplifting? Why would a President of the United States upend a brilliant career by having sex with an intern in the oval office? The world as we know it makes no sense. It is a flim-flam show, riddled with contradiction, alluring but ultimately unsatisfying.

If you are going to find healing and peace of mind, you will not find it where most people tell you to look. The visible world shows us but a tiny sliver of reality, highly distorted, like an amusement park mirror that warps your body into an image that bears little resemblance to its source. The values you have been taught to chase are not worthy guides to truth. Rather than looking outside for answers, we must look in.

Where Would You Like to Go Today?

I have often walked through the aisle of an airplane and observed hundreds of passengers watching movies on screens in front of them. Each passenger is absorbed in a movie different than the one the passenger in the next seat is watching. Likewise, you can go to a multiplex movie theater and purchase a ticket for any one of a dozen films. You can choose a drama, romance, comedy, musical, sci-fi, mystery, children's fantasy, adventure, documentary, crime, horror, or war story. When you enter the theater of your choice, you step for a few hours into the reality conjured by that tale. Even though the images you see are pure illusions, a play of light and shadows on a blank screen, they generate experiences that feel quite real. You may laugh, cry, be inspired, get scared, grow angry, or feel bored. Meanwhile people in the theater on the other side of the wall are having an entirely different experience. Then the lights come on, the movie disappears, and you return to your "real" life, which is simply a more elaborate movie.

The Internet offers an even vaster demonstration of multiple simultaneous realities. With nearly two billion websites currently online, you can tap into the entire gamut of human experience with the touch of a few keys. Without leaving your living room you can immerse yourself in shopping, politics, education, medicine, sports, gaming, dating, sex, hate, and every experience the imagination can conjure. The Internet is a fantastic teaching device to train us in the power of mind to manufacture simultaneous realities and dwell in them.

If you land on a website you find distasteful, you don't waste time and energy trying to change the website. If you do, you will become more embroiled in the thoughts, energy, and feelings you resist. If you don't like the website you are on, you switch to one you prefer and reap *that* experience. Microsoft once used a tag line, *"Where would you like to go today?"* That slogan was far closer to the truth than anyone realized.

Healing is a matter of going where you would prefer to go today. Its dynamic is as simple as switching your television channel from a depressing, disheartening movie riddled with violence and disease to a movie that lifts your soul. This is, of course, easier said than done because we have habits of thought and we make unconscious choices that keep us stuck on unrewarding channels. In a later chapter we will learn how to break those habits and make new, more conscious choices. For now, the important idea to understand is that it is possible to transition from a sickened reality to an empowering one by shifting your focus to the experience of your choice.

How to Leverage Alternate Realities for Healing

One of the most cogent proofs that simultaneous realities exist, even within one person, is Multiple Personality Disorder. People with this syndrome can display a physical disease in one personality, but no trace of the ailment in another personality. One personality could be severely allergic to citrus, and cause the person's body to break out in hives when eating an orange, while another personality could eat a basket of oranges with no side effects. One personality could be diabetic and require regular insulin injections, while in a disease-free personality the individual would be killed by the same insulin dose. One personality could show a cancer that is entirely absent in another personality. Psychologists have recently more aptly renamed this complex "Dissociative Identity Disorder," indicating that the condition is an issue of identity more than personality. This striking phenomenon leads us to a crucial question: "Can I be healed by accessing a different aspect of myself that is already healthy?"

To answer this question, consider the woman who came to the metaphysical teacher Bashar and told him that she had had a smoking habit for many years, and sorely wished to stop. She had tried many methods, but always backslid.

"Is there some other approach I could take that might work?" she asked the teacher.

Bashar explained to the woman that there are several different identities within herself she could access, which would affect if and how she stopped smoking. Within her there was a person who had always smoked, and always would. There was another person who had always smoked, but could stop with a degree of effort. Most important, there was a third person within her who had *never* smoked. If she could access and identify with the person who had never smoked, Bashar stated, she would walk the easiest path and find the most success in kicking the habit. It can't be hard to kick a habit you never had. Why would someone who had never smoked be tempted to pick up a cigarette?

The German healer Bruno Gröning helped many people become free of long-term severe addictions without withdrawal symptoms. These patients, well-documented by physicians, simply lost interest in smoking, alcohol, or hard drugs, stopped using these substances practically overnight, and did not resume the habit. Such cases demonstrate that the process of withdrawal, usually expected to be long, difficult, and painful, is not an absolute reality. It is possible to step into an altogether different reality and reap its benefits quickly.

If you are struggling to escape from a painful reality, including ill health, the first step is to realize that the reality you are experiencing is not the only reality. The second step is to recognize that you have a choice about which reality you live in. The third step is to immerse yourself in the reality you prefer instead. Focus on where you would like to go rather than what you would like to get away from. The more you talk about, complain about, identify with, and find agreement for your distasteful world, the more it will cling to you. The more you give your attention to a more desirable experience, join with others who subscribe to the same reality, and infuse consciously chosen thoughts and words to affirm it, the more real it will become to you. You always get more of what you focus on; the thought you are entertaining now is a preview of your experience to follow.

How the Beatles Produced their Greatest Work

In 1966, after becoming the most popular entertainers in history, the Beatles got fed up with concert tours. They were tired of playing their songs for crowds who wanted to scream more than listen to their music. I experienced this insanity when I attended a Beatles concert in Atlantic City. To my huge dismay, I did not hear one word of the Beatles' lyrics or music; all I heard during the entire time the band was on the stage, were fifteen thousand hysterical teenage girls yelling at the top of their lungs and crying. I can imagine how frustrating this was for a creative band like the Beatles to repeat this daunting scenario night after night.

As a result, the fab four decided to ditch concerts and go into the studio to record innovative music. Paul McCartney came up with an odd but imaginative idea: "Let's leave the old Beatles behind, completely reinvent ourselves, and become alter egos. We'll assume identities entirely discontinuous from our old selves and make a fresh statement." The band adopted the personalities of a fictitious time-warped group, "Sgt. Pepper's Lonely Hearts Club Band," and created an album filled with songs and images they plucked from the far recesses of their imagination. The Beatles spent 700 hours in the studio (compared to their usual 10) conjuring never-before-heard sounds with state-of-the-art technology, and polishing their new image. As a result, the collection became what many people consider to be the most significant album of all time, redirecting the course of popular music and influencing culture in ways that music had never achieved. I remember spending that historic summer doing little else but listening to Sgt. Pepper's.

Just as that landmark album rose from the ashes of a discarded identity, within you lie possibilities you would never dream of if you are attached to you have been rather than who you can become. Within every sick person is a healthy one yearning to come forth. Within every person struggling with finance is a lavishly opulent person waiting to claim rightful riches. Within every social misfit is a world-change agent preparing to lead the masses to better places. If you are fixated on being the outer person, you will not bring forth the inner. Every soul contains seeds of greatness. Only those who water them get to enjoy the magnificent fruits such seeds will bear for that person and many others.

Onto Higher Ground

You can't live in Manhattan and France at the same time. At any given moment you are in one place or the other. As Demi Moore's character discovered, to try to straddle both worlds will drive you mad. If you continually focus on a sick, crazy world, you will stay sick and crazy. Billions of people subscribing to painful illusions does not make them real. A large population in a mental institution does not make it sane. The spiritual journey requires a shift from the common to the uncommon; from what you have been taught to what you know; from where others have chosen to go to where you choose to go. It takes courage to claim wholeness in a world committed to fracture.

Occasionally an individual glimpses a vaster, saner reality, and shares his or her vision with others. Such people are our guides out of hell. If we gave as much attention to models of well-being as we do to dysfunctional people and situations, the world would be a far healthier place. Those who have reached higher ground extend a helping hand to those climbing behind them. This is the legacy that healers offer you, and the one you will leave for those who follow.

Eventually we will all find our way out of the valley and reach the summit. How long that takes, and how much pain we endure until that happens, is up to each of us. You can achieve a time collapse by going in thought and feeling where you wish to go before your body catches up. Leaps of faith are not a far distance when you realize that a part of you already stands where you desire to go. Come *from* healing instead of proceeding *toward* it. The realest part of you is already whole. What is whole can never be broken and what is broken can never become whole. The two realities share no common ground. You are either fragmented or unified. To accept one is to deny the other. Jesus said, "Choose this day whom you will serve," meaning, "Decide which reality you prefer to live in."

Healing is yours just on the other side of the theater wall; there is a door you can walk through. The distance from the slums to the penthouse is not far at all. Health, wealth, and happiness are not luxuries reserved for a lucky few. They are the result of intention, not circumstance, and you have access to them now. Be not deceived by the limits the world calls reality. A vaster home awaits.

MASTER KEYS *of* THIS CHAPTER

1. Many different realities comprise the universe. You live in the reality that matches your consciousness, while others live in the reality that matches their mindset.

2. You cannot experience different realities simultaneously. At any given moment you are choosing one or another.

3. The world that you have been taught is so substantial and solid, is not. Much of what the world believes to be true is false, which is why so many people suffer. To achieve healing and success, you must discern between reality and illusion.

4. You can choose the reality you experience by giving your full attention to the elements of the reality you prefer, and no attention to the elements of the reality you do not prefer.

5. If you are seeking to heal or break an undesirable habit, find and identify with the person within you who is already healed or who never had the bad habit.

6. It is possible to be healed quickly, easily, and sometimes dramatically, independent of the diagnosis or prognosis presented to you.

7. Healing and any life upgrade occur not by chance. They are the result of choices you make, first consciously, and then absorbed into your subconscious, which results in visible manifestation.

BREAK THE ROPE

I loose the world from all I thought it was.

—A Course in Miracles

Tawny is an African elephant who was captured as a baby and shipped to a circus in America. When she arrived, her trainer tied her with a rope to a stake in the ground. Young Tawny tugged at the rope, but because the stake was firmly embedded, she could not dislodge it. After a while the little elephant realized she was not going to get free from the stake, so she just accepted that she must stand within the circle the rope prescribed.

As Tawny grew, she became much stronger, to the point that if she pulled on the rope and stake firmly, she could have easily freed herself. But because she long ago accepted that the stake bound her, she did not challenge her predicament. So Tawny remained captive for many years by a shackle impotent compared to her true strength, but effectively imprisoning because she attributed undue power to it. She was confined not by her circumstances but, we might say, by her beliefs.*

---

* Lawmakers have since gained greater compassion for captive animals, and many states and countries have banned circuses from enslaving elephants and other animals for human entertainment. There are now a number of sanctuaries that provide formerly captive elephants, tigers, and other circus animals with healthy, open-space environments where they are free to live out their lives in a more natural way.

Like Tawny, you and I have been held captive by many oppressive but illusory beliefs. As children, we were taught a myriad of "facts" about sickness and health that are not true at all. These ideas have been passed down from generation to generation, underscored by worldly authorities and mass agreement, until they *appear* to be set in stone. Anna Freud, daughter of Sigmund Freud, said, "When an error becomes collective, it acquires the strength of a truth."

If you are willing to question and challenge limiting beliefs, they crumble. You were taught, for example, that people live until a certain age and then die; you will inherit the diseases that afflicted your ancestors; core childhood programming establishes your adult psychological impediments; the way to deal with diseased organs is to yank them out of your body; recovery from some illnesses or operations takes a long time or is impossible; you must depend on certain drugs or treatments for the rest of your life; uncountable diseases are lurking around the corner, from which you must constantly protect yourself; and you will suffer if you don't follow your doctor's advice.

While some of these notions and practices make sense in some situations, many of them have been pounded into us so vehemently that we hardly see our health potential clearly. What once seemed real and solid changes over time. When America first became a nation, for example, the average life expectancy was 36 years; now many people live well into their eighties and nineties, and the percentage of centenarians grows each year. George Washington died when he went to his doctor to be treated for a cold, and he asked the physician to bleed him, draining 40% of the blood from his body. When I was a child, many of my friends and I were sent to the hospital to have our tonsils removed; now many doctors cite that the tonsils play an important role in the immune system and should be left intact. A friend of mine was on the golf course a few days after his hernia surgery; now at age 70 he is an avid heli-skier; last year he skied more than in any previous year. I know people who have bounced back from a terminal cancer diagnosis and went on to live long, happy, healthy, productive lives. If there is even one exception to an apparent "law," the law is not a law; it is a belief. Real laws cannot be broken. Beliefs are regularly broken, or transcended, by people who do not subscribe to them.

Now let's look at some of the beliefs you hold that you may do well to reconsider and reprogram

I will probably live until about age _____.

[Name of disease] runs in my family or race, so I am subject to it.

I may never overcome my core psychological programming of _____ as a result of _____.

If [Name of person] hadn't done _____ to me, I wouldn't have [Name of problem.]

If I eat _____, I will have _____ reaction.

I will need to take [Name of drug or treatment] for a long time or the rest of my life.

If I am in _____ environment, I will get sick.

Doctor _____ ruined me.

Because I cannot afford _____, I cannot get healed.

Because my ex- is _____, I cannot _____.

It will probably take [length of time] for me to recover from _____.

People with a diagnosis of _____ usually die within _____.

There is no cure for _____.

Other limiting belief(s) I hold: _____.

I am not suggesting that you quit taking your medication or jump up the day after your surgery and go heli-skiing. I am suggesting that you begin to examine, question, and challenge your beliefs about health and sickness, and demand that the truth about them be revealed to you. Even saying "your beliefs" is deceptive, since "your" beliefs are not really your own. Most were adopted from other people, repeated and ingrained until you *thought* they were your own. If you were a skilled journalist, you would make it your priority to validate your sources and check the facts before you publish your story. Yet many of us write the story of our life without checking the facts that shape it.

God set up the world to work, but we must know how to work it. You cannot blame the manufacturer of a brilliant, efficient product for user error. Taking a moment to read the manual can save lots of time and trouble. I once purchased a chair I had to assemble. As I studied the instruction manual, I realized it contained errors and ambiguous information. The manual had been composed and printed in a country where English was not the native language; the steps were confusing, with unclear photos. I had to figure out how to put the chair together independent of this manual. Many of the "manuals" we have been given that supposedly guide us how to live have been written in the language of fear and separation, foreign to our true nature. The pictures we have been shown about how to find happiness are contradictory and confusing. If we try to put our lives together using these manuals, they won't work. Meanwhile there is a greater manual, based on universal principles, that will yield us phenomenal well-being when we follow its instructions.

Greater than Ghosts

My beloved Dee and I have the joy of living with a family of wonderful dogs. While our fur kids are almost always cuddly, loving, and fun, they sometimes display primal dog instincts, like a pecking order. One dog, Marley, used to growl at his brother Henry when Henry approached Henry's food bowl near Marley's, so Henry kept his distance. To keep the peace, we placed Henry's bowl in another room, where he ate without his brother bugging him. Eventually Marley went home to heaven, and we placed Henry's food bowl back with the rest of the family. Yet Henry still feared to approach his bowl, and sat off to the side. Even though Marley was no longer around to intimidate Henry, the memory stopped him.

Many of us block ourselves from receiving healing because we are intimidated by a fear or threat that is long gone. We let ghosts deter us. I heard about a man who rode a horse that once tripped over a tree stump on a dirt road. The man had the stump removed, but every time the horse approached the place the stump had been, he was spooked and tried to turn back. He missed an enjoyable ride because he was running from a ghost.

If you are living at less than your full potential, you may be running from the ghost of something that happened long ago or something you fear will happen. You may also accept the ghosts of other people's experiences and allow them to infiltrate your mind. Yet who you are is greater than any ghost or demon. With our encouragement, Henry overcame his fear and now he eats happily with the rest of the family. If our dog can defeat his ghostly fear, so can you. You are an expression of God, and nothing in the universe is more powerful than God.

When the quest for reality becomes more important than clinging to fear, truth reveals itself. In 1988 the Soviet Union cancelled the history final exams for 50 million students because the history they had been taught was built largely on lies. Much of the history we have been taught, especially about our limits, is also based on lies. When we shine the light on them, they dissolve into the nothingness from which they came.

When you realize that your limits do not belong to you, you can begin to disown them and release yourself from the power they have held over you. All limits exist only in your mind, and that is the place where they must be healed. Topical cures can help, but in the long run you must uproot illness at its source. I often quote Thoreau: "There are a thousand hacking at the branches of evil to one who is striking at the root." We can spend years hacking at the symptoms of disease, but until we address its cause, it will persist. But disease and loss do not define you. You are an infinite, limitless, eternal, whole, perfect, deathless spirit. All of your experiences are leading you to that golden awareness. You were not born to perform in a circus to entertain small-minded living. A greater destiny calls.

MASTER KEYS *of* THIS CHAPTER

1. All limits are learned as a result of erroneous programming. As an expression of a whole and perfect God, you are unlimited and free.

2. A large number of people participating in an illusion does not make the illusion true.

3. "Your" beliefs about limitations are not really yours. They were adopted from other people, and have nothing to do with your true self or divine potential.

4. The history of humanity demonstrates over and over again that what once seemed impossible, is possible.

5. Any disease can be healed. Many people have been healed of diseases that have been called unhealable.

6. To break free of a disease or limit, hold it up to the light and allow a higher truth to dissolve the false beliefs that have kept it in force.

7. The fears and roadblocks that stop us are but ghosts of past limiting thoughts. When we face our issues here and now with a clear, courageous, and willing mind, they disappear and we are free to move ahead.

FROM NORMAL
TO NATURAL

Everyone has a doctor in him or her;
we just have to help it in its work.

The natural healing force within each one of us
is the greatest force in getting well.

—HIPPOCRATES

One afternoon my mother sent me to the supermarket to buy some applesauce on sale. As I perused the bottles on the shelf I found an intriguing ad for the product: "Food-town Applesauce: $1.99—*Natural or Regular.*"

I checked the labels. The regular applesauce contained sugar, artificial coloring, chemical preservatives, and other ingredients that do not come with apples from a tree. The natural applesauce, on the other hand, contained only apples and water.

What is normal isn't always natural. To the contrary, the normal often denies or defies the natural. If you wish to be healed, you will need to let go of the normal and return to the natural.

While healing may seem to be one of the hardest things to achieve, it is the most natural and does not require struggle. Struggle is stressful, and works against healing. You don't have to fight to be healed. People often talk about "battling cancer." While I understand the concept and I totally support anyone seeking to be healed of cancer or any disease, I suggest reframing the process. Fighting anything depletes you. Aligning with your goal empowers you. Instead of battling a disease, align with wellness. What is natural is more powerful than what is unnatural. Nature is an expression of Source. Health is natural. Disease is not.

You may be tempted to argue that disease is a part of life. Disease is rampant in nature. Everyone gets sick at some time. When you get sick enough, you die. That's the way is. But, as I noted in the last chapter, there is more than one way that it is. Appearances indicate one "is," while a higher reality indicates another "is." When we align with a higher reality, we reap its benefits.

I hired a real estate agent to sell my house. After a few months without a sale, he sent me an email itemizing all the things wrong with the property. He concluded by saying, "I don't mean to be negative. I am just telling it like it is." I thanked him for his honesty and took him off the job. I told him sincerely, "I don't want to put you in the position of trying to sell a house you don't have confidence in."

I hired another realtor who loved the house and highlighted all of its positive qualities to me and prospective buyers. She sold the place in short order. She also told it like it is, but she chose a different "is" to tell it like.

Take care which "is" you are telling it like. You will reap the results of the "is" you focus on. You can argue for your illness or your healing, and each argument will take you to more of the same. In his brilliant book *Illusions*, Richard Bach states, "Argue for your limitations, and sure enough they're yours." Henry Ford said, "Think you can or think you can't, and either way you will be correct."

Ultimately nature, positivity, and well-being are far more real "is's" than unnatural living, negativity, and illness.

Light is more powerful than darkness. When the two meet, light prevails.

From the Unreal to the Real

Disease is not of God. God did not create disease. God does not experience disease. God does not know disease. God does not want you to be sick. God does not see you as sick. God wants only your well-being. Disease is the result of erroneous thinking and exists only in a skewed reality. If you live in a reality where disease is real and powerful, you have strayed from the natural world. Many spiritual paths such as Advaita Vedanta, Christian Science, and Unity affirm the fundamental benevolence of creation. Practitioners refuse to get involved in disease thinking. Even while patients present their ailments, the practitioner holds the high watch and remembers the patient's wholeness even in the face of the appearance of disease.

Joel Goldsmith was a brilliant metaphysical teacher and healer who established a path he called The Infinite Way. He wrote many insightful books and taught generously and prolifically. I am told that when people came to Goldsmith for healing, they did not meet him in person. The patient sat in Goldsmith's living room while Goldsmith sat in a small room off to the side and prayed for that person. He was not interested in hearing about their symptoms. His only job was to establish himself in knowing their perfect well-being. While his patients had become immersed in the normal world, Goldsmith remained founded in the natural world. As a result, he had a high rate of healing.

You, too, can achieve healing for yourself and others by staying with the natural. Ask your inner guidance to help you distinguish between the pure world of vitality and the twisted world of disease. The Hindu prayer known as the Pamavana Mantra captures this distinction:

> Lead me from the unreal to the real.
>
> Lead me from darkness to light.
>
> Lead me from the temporary to the immortal.

The Healing Stream

A mighty river of life flows generously and endlessly through the entire universe. Lao Tse called it "the Tao," or "the Great Way." More recently George Lucas dubbed it "the Force." Yogis call it *prana*. The Chinese call it *chi*. Hawaiians call it *mana*. This invisible yet very real energy animates everything that lives. Like the wind, you cannot see it, but it has potent effects. The key to healing is to align with the healing stream and let it work for you and through you.

When we step out of alignment with life force, beginning with erroneous thinking, things start to go wrong. Our body breaks down, our finances stall, and our relationships grow turbulent. What was created to be delightful becomes a disaster.

We can return to the stream by regaining alignment. Quit doing what pulls you out of the flow, and cultivate thoughts and activities that immerse you in it. Do not be shy or apologetic about doing what makes you happy. No one has the right to judge your stream, and you don't have the right to judge others' streams. I had lunch with a fellow who enjoys the hobby of restoring military aircraft. While I would find such a pursuit quite boring, this man's passion for his craft was contagious. I thoroughly enjoyed listening to him because of the exuberant energy behind his words. His hobby brought him life, which spilled over to me. Behold the healing power that life force delivers when we harness it. Your passion enlivens you and anyone in your sphere of influence. You probably know some people in whose presence you always feel good. They are tapped into the stream, and you are catching the overflow. You, too, are such an uplifter when you are aligned with the magnificent "Is."

> *I go to nature to be soothed, healed,*
> *and have my senses put in order.*

> —JOHN BURROUGHS

The Great Return

In the classic movie *Lost Horizon* (1939 version), statesman Robert Conway and his brother are kidnapped to Shangri-La, a mystical utopian community tucked deep in the Himalayas. In Shangri-La the weather is perfect, people live in harmony, and they enjoy disease-free lifespans of hundreds of years. There Conway finds tranquility he has never known in the turbulent world he left behind. He falls in love with a radiant woman, and his life becomes a glorious expression of well-being, far more than he has ever known. Then Conway's brother convinces him that the community is fake and the two must flee. Conway tearfully leaves Shangri-La and his lover, and returns to the "real" world, which he finds terribly brutal by contrast. Eventually he realizes that his brother lied to him; Shangri-La was far closer to reality than anything the artificial world has manufactured. Conway then has to fight his way through rugged mountains, blizzards, and awful hardships to get back to paradise. When he finally arrives at Shangri-La, he owns it because he recognizes its reality and he was willing to do whatever it took to claim it.

People who find ways to heal from a disease appreciate their health and life far more than if they had not been sick. They savor every moment of life and value their relationships far more than if they had not been threatened. I have heard people say, "Looking back, I see how that experience had to happen to motivate me to achieve a powerful course correction." Such people use their disease to pivot and build health by choice. Like Conway who forged his way back to paradise, they are now aligned with their well-being by choice.

When you were born you were given a generous bank account of life force. How you manage that account determines your health and happiness. You don't have to do anything to earn health; it is your natural inheritance. You just have to quit doing things that work against your life force and deplete it. If you squander your energy or invest it in self-defeating activities, your balance will run into the red, which we call disease. You can have a strong stream of water running into a bathtub, but if the drain is unplugged, the water will run out. Plug the drain, and you will have an abundant supply of water. Realign with life force, and healing follows naturally.

When you rest at night, God makes a new deposit in your life force account. Even if you invested yesterday's portion unwisely by engaging in thoughts, feelings, and actions that ran your battery down, you are renewed; you can start over and make more empowering choices for the new day. Such is the miracle of grace. God loves us so much that He is willing to keep investing in us. *A Course in Miracles* asks us to remember, "I am sustained by the love of God," and "By grace I live. By grace I am released."

Take a moment now to consider how you are managing your life force account:

What I do that increases my life force	What I do that diminishes my life force
_____	_____
_____	_____
_____	_____
_____	_____
_____	_____
_____	_____
_____	_____
_____	_____

Your answers to the above list map your prescription for healing. Do what brings you life and quit doing what deadens you. All religions, spiritual paths, gurus, consciousness trainings, mentors, teachers, and sacred texts are based on the maintenance, expression, and expansion of life force. Seek no further. Take the express train to healing by living true to what brings you life. All else is detail.

Don't be a Good Patient

My friend Dr. Michael Klaper is one of the world's foremost authorities on vegan nutrition. He has helped many people heal by teaching them how to shift toward a plant-based diet. Dr. Klaper was invited to speak at a conference on diabetes. "Before my lecture, an educator gave a talk on 'How to be a Good Diabetes Patient,'" Dr. Klaper recounted. "She gave patients a strict regimen to follow in order to keep their diabetes in check. When I went onstage, I explained to the audience that I did not want them to be good diabetes patients. I wanted them to be free of diabetes. Why would you put up with a disease you can cure by changing your diet? I don't want patients to simply accommodate to their disease. I want them to heal it."

Dr. Klaper points us to a crucial reframe: Don't accept disease as a fact of life. It may be a normal fact, but it is not a natural fact. French genius mathematician, physicist, and inventor Blaise Pascal declared, "There are truths on this side of the Pyrenees, which are falsehoods on the other." The fact that many people agree that certain diseases are incurable, or take a long time to cure, does not make it a truth. If even one person has been healed of a certain disease, it cannot be called incurable.

What other people do with their diseases does not have anything to do with what you do with your health. Statistics document what the masses do, but they do not account for individuals who choose a different path. Withdraw your attention from the reality that others choose, and focus on the one you would choose. A friend of mine was diagnosed with a certain disease. Her son told me, "as soon as my mom was diagnosed, I did intensive research on that disease. I want to know exactly what we were dealing with." While the son's intentions were sincere, his method was flawed. His research did not educate him as to what he and his mom were dealing with. His research educated him as to how other people dealt with the same disease. Each patient applied his or her unique mindset to the disease, for better or worse. If you are going to "know what you are dealing with," study the people who were healed of that disease, not the ones who succumbed to it. Ultimately you are addressing your thoughts about a disease. When you heal your thoughts about a disease, you are in the best possible position to heal the disease.

A Global Reset

The coronavirus pandemic served the monumental function of pointing humanity toward a global reset. Just as a challenging disease can move an individual to create a life-changing course correction, the pandemic forced nearly the entire population of Planet Earth to reconsider how we are living. While the pandemic tragically led to many deaths, financial losses, and social disruptions, many people extracted important life lessons. Here are some of them:

We were forced to stop and take pause from the frenzied and in many ways meaningless activities that often characterize our lives, including ceaselessly working, dashing here and there to buy more stuff, and pursuing goals that leave us wanting. Instead, we could get quiet, reflect, and be with ourselves. The journey outward became a journey inward.

We were given the gift of quality time with our families and loved ones. How many people complain that we wish we had more time to be home with our spouse, children, and pets? The quarantine time allowed us to connect with the people most important to us, communicate, and affirm our most meaningful relationships. One woman told me, "I sat on the porch and had a two-hour conversation with my 14-year-old son. That would never have happened otherwise." Another told me, "I have not gotten along with my parents for a long time. Being with them intimately and intensively forced old issues to the surface, which we faced and healed. Now I love and appreciate my parents more than ever."

Many of us were moved to rethink our careers and goals, and reinvent ourselves. Some people lost their jobs, and told more truth about what they would rather be doing. Some established visions and plans for new vocational directions. Many people worked remotely from home rather than commuting to an office, and decided they would prefer this to be their lifestyle rather than driving in traffic to a sterile, often toxic workplace.

Many people used their unexpected free time for spiritual growth. They meditated, prayed, did yoga, read inspiring books, watched videos, and participated in online meetings and courses on subjects fulfilling to their souls. Had they remained immersed in their usual routines, they would have been too busy to take care of their inner being.

The miracle of online technology enabled us to recognize that we are all connected and we can communicate deeply and richly, even if our bodies are in different places. Geography cannot separate us. When we are joined in spirit, we are truly together.

For the first time in history, all of humanity was joined in a common cause: heal from the pandemic. The virus leveled the playing field; we were all in the situation equally. Covid-19 did not make the distinctions we usually use to judge and separate. It affected people of all ages, genders, religions, nations, financial status, social position, and worldly success. England's Prince Charles and Prime Minister Boris Johnson tested positive, as did top-tier actor Tom Hanks and his wife Rita Wilson. All the ways we usually fabricate unreal, painful hierarchies, dissolved.

Many people reached out to help one another in ways we would never have considered had times been easier. A man in Australia was passing by a long line of out-of-work people waiting for public financial assistance. He went to his bank, withdrew $10,000, and gave each person in line a $100 bill. People stood on balconies near hospitals and cheered for medical workers as they went to and from work. Flight crews in England, unable to fly, set up hospitality rooms in hospitals to refresh workers on break. A policeman found a woman lurking at the rear window of a nursing home, trying to see her husband whom she was unable to visit. The policeman went to a local electronics store and got the manager to donate an iPad to both spouses so they could communicate. An off-work woman in Portugal discovered two elderly people in her apartment building who needed help. She shopped and cooked for them, and drove them to medical appointments. The pandemic proved the adage, "People are like teabags. When we get into hot water, our true strength comes forth."

The Planet Earth experienced a Sabbath. With people staying home, the environment had a chance to heal and give us a vision of the world God created rather than the one we messed up. Satellite photos showed that the terrible pollution over Chinese cities had disappeared. People in India saw the Himalayan Mountains clearly at a distance of 100 miles, for the first time in 30 years. In Hawaii, fish and ocean wildlife began to repopulate offshore areas where human activity has run them off at beaches. Coral reefs began to come back to life. For the first time in our lifetimes, we remembered how clean, clear, and life-sustaining the world can be if we respect and cooperate with it.

Like a personal disease, a planetary disease pushed us to the edge and forced us to fly. While the losses sustained by the pandemic were disastrous and heartbreaking, the insights gained by those who chose to find them were remarkable. If the world becomes a better place in any way because of what we learned, humanity has grown. The experience was an epic reminder that it's not what happens that makes or breaks our life. It's what we make of it.

A True Homecoming

All disease, personal or planetary, is a call for us to reclaim our natural state. It beckons us to reclaim our natural state of mind, which leads us to our natural state of body. Illness is a red flag guiding us to make a needed course correction. An illness is not a dead end. It is an arrow pointing in a better direction. Like the prodigal son, we have all wandered in a far country and found the journey to be long and unfulfilling. But that's not the end of the story. It is but one chapter that leads to a more fulfilling conclusion.

Like the father of the prodigal son, God is overjoyed to welcome you home, no matter how far away or for how long you have wandered. The moment you take even a small step in the direction of healing, Higher Power will rush to your assistance and provide the means for the remaining steps. Nature will always have its way. We can do all kinds of bizarre things to override nature or try to twist what is natural into what is normal, but eventually all of life reverts to the way it is rather than the way we made it. Below and behind all the changes the physical world displays, our natural state as whole divine beings remains intact. This is the true homecoming.

MASTER KEYS *of* THIS CHAPTER

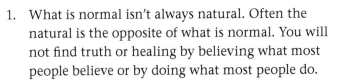

1. What is normal isn't always natural. Often the natural is the opposite of what is normal. You will not find truth or healing by believing what most people believe or by doing what most people do.

2. Healing is easy because you are returning to your natural state and accepting God's will for your well-being.

3. Instead of fighting disease, align with wellness. Your natural state is more powerful than your adopted state. When darkness meets light, light prevails.

4. When you "tell it like it is," be sure you tell it like love created it, not the "is" that fear fabricated.

5. God did not create disease and God does not maintain it. God knows only perfect wellness.

6. You do not need to know the facts about a disease to heal it. You need to know the truth about healing.

7. Life Force is the real healer. All healing proceeds from universal principles established by God.

8. People who find ways to heal from a disease usually appreciate their health and life more than if they had not been sick. They own their wellness because they have participated in it.

9. Every day you have a new opportunity to claim healing, regardless of your history.

10. You stimulate healing by recognizing what brings you life and doing it; and recognizing what diminishes your life force and ceasing to do that.

11. Don't be a "good patient." Be a healed patient

12. Disease is not a punishment. It is a wake-up call for us to return to our natural state.

YOUR RIGHT TO BE HEALED

You are not a beggar at the table of life.
You are the honored guest.

— EMMANUEL/PAT RODEGAST

Entitlement is a hot topic these days. Many people are claiming their right to receive money, government benefits, family inheritances, land, education, better treatment from the opposite sex, respect for their culture, and more. While many of these goals are worth pursuing, there is one far more important entitlement that most people overlook, and settle for far less: the right to vibrant health. You deserve to have a body that works well. Feeling good is not too much to ask for. It is the very least you should settle for.

I was invited to address a conference of social workers who met at a convention center with a casino. One afternoon I tried my hand at gambling. I was fascinated to overhear conversations among other gamblers. "How'd you make out?" one fellow asked another at a roulette table. "Not so good. I'm down five hundred dollars." At the craps table: "Did you win anything?" "No, but I'm not doing too bad. Lost just two-fifty." At the slot machines: "How is lady luck treating you?" "Okay, I guess. A hundred bucks in the hole."

I was amazed that the mark of success was not how much folks had won, but about little they had lost.

Many of us approach our health and prosperity with the same deficit mindset. If we can just make ends meet or minimize our losses, we believe we are doing well. Life becomes more about damage control than creative, productive expression. There is a world of difference between trying to fill a black hole and living from vibrant supply. Each state of mind marks an entirely different reality and begets more of the same. Thinking "deficiency" leads to more deficiency. Thinking "prosperity" leads to more prosperity. I repeat: you always get more of whatever you focus on. You cannot get to health by focusing on illness. You get to health only by focusing on health.

Your Royal Right

We relate to God by assuming one of several identities: (1) a **beggar** who does not deserve good on his own merit, and pleads for mercy; (2) a **servant** who must constantly work to earn God's favor; and (3) a **child of God** who lives in the royal estate and deserves all the rights, riches, and privileges of the kingdom.

If you believe you are a beggar, you have no entitlement. "Beggars can't be choosers," so you plead for scraps and leftovers and take what you can get. If you regard yourself as a servant, you must constantly earn your keep and avoid doing anything that ruffles your boss's feathers. A child of God, by contrast, deserves all the benefits of the kingdom simply by virtue of her identity. She does not have to prove herself or earn her good. She was born into royalty, and that is her undeniable destiny. Everything her parents have is hers because of who she is.

When you know who you are, you know what you deserve. Quit pleading for your good or trying to justify it. Instead, claim it. If you had a winning lottery ticket, you would not go to the lottery office and apologize for your unworthiness to collect your winnings. Nor would you ask, "What work do I have to do to receive my check?" You would present your ticket and the agent would hand you your check. In a sense, you have already won the lottery. The winnings are not simply money, but abundance in every form, including vibrant health. Our wealth is already given; God is just waiting for us to receive and enjoy it. Jesus delivered this lesson in many ways: "Ask, and you shall receive." "It is the Father's good pleasure to give you the kingdom." "I have come to bring you life more abundant." How many times do we need to hear the truth before we live it?

Your True Bloodline

The publication of *The DaVinci Code* and similar books stimulated a heated controversy about the bloodline of Jesus Christ. According to these books, Jesus Christ had a child or children, whose bloodline can be traced to this day. A handful of people are designated as the offspring of Jesus.

This intriguing idea captures a seed of truth and stirs a pot of distraction. The seed of truth is that, spiritually speaking, we are *all* the descendants of Christ, or Yahweh, or Allah, or whatever name you assign Higher Power. Your soul was created by God and you remain an eternal expression of Perfect Spirit. No matter your physical genetics, your nature is inextinguishable light. The pot of distraction is that physical genetics determine our divine nature. Here we get mired substituting material conditions for spiritual reality. Regardless of our physical bloodline, we are *all* heirs to the kingdom. Don't be distracted by biology. Be enamored with divinity. The flesh and the spirit tell two very different stories. Take care not to confuse the two.

Prerequisites for Healing

The world prescribes endless tasks we must accomplish before we deserve to be healed. Physically we must change our diet, take medicine or vitamin supplements, work out, lose weight, find the right doctor, move to a healthier environment, and more. Emotionally we must overcome childhood traumas, manage our upsets, forgive our ex, accept people we can't stand, and more. Spiritually, we must be kinder to others, meditate, pray, go to church, give to charity, read the scriptures, accept a particular religious leader as our savior, proselytize others, and more.

All of these methods work if you believe in them. If such practices bring you reward, please continue; many of them form habits that create a healthy, happy life. Yet there is one fundamental prerequisite for wellness that runs deeper than all the others: You must know your right to be healthy. *A Course in Miracles* tells us, "Miracles are everyone's right, but purification is necessary first." Such purification refers partly to the body, but mostly to the mind. What's the use of fasting or doing yoga if your mind is spinning in fear? If you can get out of fear and into love, you end up where prayer and fasting are designed to take you. When you drop into deep self-worth, healing follows naturally.

Whether you are seeking physical healing, financial abundance, or a stellar relationship, the first step is to know that you deserve it. Now. Here. Just as you are. Before you jump through any more hoops. What is outrageous is not what you ask for. What is outrageous is what you settle for.

Refuse to tolerate any sense of "not-enoughness" or "maybe one day." God created you sufficient in every way; nothing you can do can deny or detract from your magnificence. Replace your belief in unworthiness with deep knowing of your unspeakable preciousness, and your world will rearrange itself in amazing synchronistic ways.

Let Your Body Speak Your Mind

Richard Bach said, "Your body is your thoughts in a form you can see." Unhealed situations represent unhealed thoughts. Healed situations represent right thinking. Quit entertaining thoughts that tell you that you deserve illness, poverty, or disharmony, or that you must put up with pain or loss. Instead, welcome only thoughts of your absolute wellness. You would not allow a thief or murderer into your house, so why would you allow one into your mind? Self-demeaning thoughts steal your joy and suffocate your dreams. Self-honoring thoughts affirm your right to the kingdom, spiritually and physically. When you see yourself as God sees you, your body will reconfigure to reflect your higher vision.

Instead of demanding your good, command it. Demanding proceeds from a sense of fear and lack. You believe that someone else has the power to withhold your supply, so you cast yourself as a victim and battle for your rights. With such a mindset, your power to manifest your desired result is minimal. What proceeds from fear must backfire. What proceeds from self-knowing must succeed. Use your God-given power to command health, wealth, and love. A Roman centurion came to Jesus and requested healing for his servant. When Jesus offered to come to his home, the centurion refused, saying, "In my position of authority, I give men orders and they snap to it. I know that if you speak the word, my servant will be healed." Jesus was touched and replied, "I have not found such great faith even in Israel." When the centurion went home, he found his servant healed.

When you ask for healing, you are invoking the power that spun the stars into the heavens. Lesser powers may seem to challenge the will of God, and may appear to temporarily prevail, but ultimately they are impotent. Only the creations of light are real. *A Course in Miracles* tells us, "You are entitled to miracles." Ask not just for what you want, but what you deserve. Speak, act, and live like the child of a king or queen. Never snivel or apologize. Stand in the dignity in which you were created, and the universe will lay at your feet the holy gifts you richly deserve.

MASTER KEYS *of* THIS CHAPTER

1. You are entitled to healing and all the good things that life has to offer. Settling for anything less is an unnecessary compromise.

2. Life is not about simply surviving, offsetting a deficit, or damage control. It is about thriving and enjoying the gifts and blessings laid before us.

3. A "beggar" or "servant" mentality does not befit you. When you step into your identity as a child of God, you gain access to the kingdom God created for your fulfillment.

4. Your spiritual heritage far transcends physical biology. Your true bloodline is royal. All that God is, you are. All that God owns is yours. All that God can do, you can do.

5. The fundamental prerequisite for healing is a change of mind. When your mind changes, everything changes.

6. Your body is a communication device that gives you messages about what your mind is doing. The body becomes your friend when it teaches you to correct your mind.

7. Instead of *demanding* your good, *command* it.

LIFE BEYOND LABELS

Definitions belong to the definers, not the defined.

—Toni Morrison

You have been taught that if you name something, you gain power over it. Yet this principle backfires when we become so fixated on giving things names that they gain power over us. The title of a book by Carlin Diamond brilliantly captures this principle: *Love It, Don't Label It.* In an era of obsession with categories and endless dissection of life into tiny pieces, we can use more love and fewer tags.

The field of medicine is masterful at labeling diseases, for many good reasons. Yet when we seek to heal a disease, thinking in boxes can work against us. We treat the disease as a thing that has a life of its own rather than an energy stream that has become blocked. Quantum physicists argue over whether an observed phenomenon is a particle or a wave; is it a thing, or a flow? An object, or an energy? While there are arguments on both sides, we do far better to think of a disease as trapped or disordered energy rather than an independent entity.

When we observe symptoms—even the word "symptom" is an interpretation—our mind tends to jump to what disease this phenomenon might be heralding. Medical students often go into a tizzy when they notice symptoms in their bodies associated with the many diseases they are studying. Hypochondriacs do the same. The mind focused on disease is constantly gathering evidence to support its reality. So is the mind focused on health.

A number of my coaching clients are medical doctors. The most consistent complaint I hear about their profession is that they hate the paperwork they have to submit. One doctor spends one-third of his working hours seeing patients, and two-thirds filling out forms. A psychiatrist must document in detail her conversations with her patients, so she sits with a laptop between her and the patient, constantly typing rather than engaging with the patient eye-to-eye. Why the deluge of papers and labels? Doctors cannot get paid by insurance companies, the primary source of their income, unless they assign a diagnosis to a patient. To maintain their livelihood, physicians must put every patient in a box.

But what if a client does not fit into a box? What if there is more to a patient than their current complaint, and their potential for healing exceeds the name of their disease? What if a client's physical symptoms are more related to their mental and emotional matrix than external influences? What if the physician's vision of the patient is a major factor in the patient's healing, and can generate transformation beyond medication?

While doctors may need to label patients for professional and financial purposes, the real damage occurs when patients adopt those labels and identify with them. Rather than thinking, "I have this issue I am addressing," most patients tend to *become* their diagnosis. "I am a diabetic." "I am a schizophrenic." "I am a cancer patient." While all of these identities have practical implications in treatment, the leap from "I have" to "I am" is monumental and in many cases tragic. Metaphysically, the words "I am" are the most powerful that a human being can utter. They represent the word of God becoming manifest in form. "In the beginning was the word" applies not only to the beginning of the universe, but to the beginning of every human endeavor. Whatever you fill in the blank with after you say, "I am," you create in your experience. If you truly wish to be healed and lead a healthy, productive life, take extreme care when choosing the words following, "I am," for in speaking them you build your destiny.

The Old and New Testaments underscore the power of these two mighty words. When Moses encountered God at the summit of Mount Sinai, he asked, "What shall I tell the people that your name is?" God replied, "I am that I am." Because God's name is "I am," whenever you speak those words you invoke the creative power of God.

When Jesus was asked who he was, he answered, "I am the way, the truth, and the life." Jesus identified only with the attributes of God, which are equally true of all of us. Jesus did not claim his religion, gender, family, or body as himself. He claimed the highest that he was, as a model for all of us to follow. Jesus' mission was not to set himself up as an idol to be worshipped, but as a wayshower to inspire us to accept the divine identity we share with him.

Toss the Folder

Psychologist Dr. William Parker used unusual healing methods to obtain extraordinary results. He refused to identify his patients with their medical history. Dr. Parker was asked to treat a young man with a long record of drug addiction, who was directed to him because a string of doctors had failed to relieve him of his habit. The fellow walked into the doctor's office with a stack of manila folders under his arm, dossiers of all his unsuccessful treatments. He set the pile on the psychologist's desk and began to explain his addiction.

Without a word, Dr. Parker shoved the folders off the desktop into a trash can. "Now tell me who you are without your addiction. What did you do this week that was not addictive?"

That request catapulted this troubled young man in an entirely new direction. Instead of focusing on the addict, the therapist focused on the empowered person. Dr. Parker developed his relationship with his patient on that baseline, and over time he was the only professional who was able to help free this young man of his debilitating habit.

If you are a healing practitioner or you simply want to help your friends, don't pigeonhole your clients or friends into their diagnosis or their history. If you know their issue, you can certainly offer ways to help. Meanwhile remember that they are a dynamic, fluid, spiritual being, with the capacity to be new every day, and the power to rise beyond past labels and limits. What we call "reality" is not solid at all. It is fluent, more like a river than a rock. We are more energy than matter. Our bodies and personalities are a result of how we are moving our life force or stifling it. Even a slight change in the direction you are flowing your energy can create startling results.

One day I was sitting on my lawn watching cloud formations float by. At one point I saw a cloud in the perfect shape of a French Poodle. The formation was so stunning that I wanted to capture it in a photo. I dashed into my house, grabbed my phone, and returned to shoot the picture. By that time the cloud had dissolved and bore little resemblance to the poodle. My entire trip into the house didn't take more than a minute. In that short time the wind had blown the formation apart. I regard the experience as a lesson in the amorphous and impermanent nature of the physical world.

All things in form are dynamic more than they are static, including your body. We want to believe the world is stationary because the idea gives us a sense of security; we hold the illusion that we can control the world by locking it into a position. But it is not so. Everything is always moving.

Allow for your patients, friends, and yourself to re-form disease to health; longtime patterns into fresh possibilities. When you wake up in the morning, you are not the same person who went to sleep last night—unless you choose to drag yesterday's identity into the new day. No matter what disease you had yesterday, how long you have had a particular ailment, or the prognosis your doctor gave you, today you are brand new and you can choose a new experience. "Behold, I make all things new." Nothing has to be the way it has been. If you like the way it has been, carry on. If you do not like what you have created, you are free to create something new.

Don't superimpose what was onto what is. Don't talk about your history of disease; complain about your past ailments, doctors, or treatments; or talk about the people you know who had that disease and what happened to them. Today be resurrected from the tomb of dark memories and projections. Have you ever thought about why, when you sleep, your pain goes away? During slumber your consciousness departs from your body, including its ills. If you injured your ankle, the ankle hurts until you go to sleep. While you sleep, it doesn't bother you. Yet it's the same ankle in the same condition it was in when you fell asleep minutes earlier. Now it doesn't hurt at all. That's because you removed your attention from it. Your experience has a lot more to do with where you mind is focused than what your body is doing. When you withdraw your mind from the injury, you ceased to associate fearful, pained thoughts with the ankle, and in that refreshing space it has a chance to heal. When you wake up, the ankle feels better. The Apostle Paul said, "Be renewed by the renewing of the mind." If you attempt to renew your body without renewing your mind, the results will be nil or short lived. When you renew the mind, healing follows. The body is not the cause of the mind. All manifestation proceeds from thought. This is why it is so important to be vigilant about the thoughts you indulge and entertain.

Give your Friends a Break

Just as you can help heal yourself by not identifying with a disease or harping on it, you can contribute to your friends' healing by not freezing them into their illnesses or problems. Don't keep asking them how their arthritis is, talking to them about people who also have allergies, passing along news stories about the latest research on depression, or pointing to where your back hurts like theirs. If they are in pain and you can help them, certainly do. Otherwise don't bring up the subject unless they do. And do not tell other people about your friend's disease unless you have permission and a good reason. Gossip hurts.

I used to get together a few times a year with my friend Tom, a 40-something therapist from Philadelphia. At the time, Tom was recently divorced and he was dating different women. Over a period of several years he had a number of girlfriends. When we met for dinner, he would bring his current partner, different than the one he had introduced the previous year. When Tom finally settled into a long-term relationship, he told me, "I want to thank you for your support while I was dating. I know I introduced you to a bunch of different women, and I felt embarrassed; that was a confusing phase for me. Yet you always accepted me and the person I was with as if we were the real deal. You never said, 'Whatever happened to Susan?' or 'I liked Janet better' or 'Why can't you sustain a relationship?' While other people criticized me as being fickle or a womanizer, you always accepted me in the moment, you never locked me into my past, and you let me be new. Thank you for seeing the best in me and supporting me as I grew in my relationships."

We draw forth the best in others when we focus on what is right with them rather than harping on their faults, pains, or illnesses. If you truly want to help someone heal, see them as healed and speak to their wellness rather than their illness. You might be the only person in their life who sees them as whole, empowered, and new. As such, you serve as a life saver. You would not want people to cast a net over you by identifying you with what is or was wrong with you, so offer your loved ones the same kindness and respect.

Love without Conditions

Once while I was dealing with some ongoing physical pain, I went to my buddy Fred's house, where we were to meet some friends to go hiking. When they arrived, Fred told the other guys, "I don't know if Alan will join us. He is dealing with a condition."

When Fred described me as having a condition, something inside me went "thud." I didn't think of myself as having a condition. A part of my body was simply temporarily weakened. Fred turned it into a condition, which felt far more burdensome. I consciously rejected Fred's limiting image of me. Eventually the pain disappeared. I was glad that I didn't accept Fred's "condition," or the experience may have gone on longer than it did.

A disease, like all other elements of your experience, represents an idea you are holding. We live more in the world of ideas than things. If you face a health issue, think of it as an idea you are holding. Just as you took hold of an idea, you can let it go. Ideas are not as solid as things. A "condition" implies that your well-being has become conditional on something outside you. But there is another level of well-being that is unconditional. You have the power to choose wellness independent of external conditions. As a spiritual being, your body is external to you. When you realize that the world lives in your mind more than you live in the world, you have attained the first step of spiritual mastery.

What's Your Story?

You can become so entrenched in a story about your illness that it becomes a snare that entraps you. "I've had this bum back for years." "Doctors can't figure out what's wrong with me." "My ex is a constant pain in the butt." When you rehearse and rehash a medical, financial, or relationship problem, you limit your chances to release yourself from it.

In some of my seminars I lead an exercise called "My Ideal Day." I ask participants to write out in detail their idea of a perfect day, including only desirable elements. Then they read their description to the group. One lady read aloud her ideal day and concluded, ". . . and then my husband and I go to the opera in Toronto. We rent a long limousine so he can stretch out his arthritic legs."

Hearing that, an alarm sounded in my head. "Why would you include arthritic legs in an ideal day?" I had to ask her.

She thought for a moment and answered, "I guess it's because he has had arthritis for so long that it's hard for me to imagine him without it."

This woman's essay was not really about her ideal day; it was about a compromised day. To be healed, we must confront the stories we tell ourselves and others about what isn't working. When you think of a situation as a fact of life, it tends to remain so. When you question and challenge the idea that this is just the way it is, and consider how good it could get instead, you open the door to changing it for the better.

Be very aware of the stories you tell, and delete those that represent conditions you do not wish to continue. When you define yourself by a certain illness, you reinforce it. Abraham (of Abraham-Hicks) states that when a disease is diagnosed, its symptoms exacerbate. When you think or talk about yourself as having that disease, you tap into the mindset of everyone who has ever had that disease, what doctors think about it, and the results patients have obtained. Thoughts are things and forces. They ripple out into the universe and form clouds in the psyche of humanity. Ernest Holmes, founder of Science of Mind, called this pool "race thought," the collective thoughts of the human race. Because humanity's predominant thoughts tend to be fear-based, when you tap into race thought you are generally tapping into a negative consciousness. Dark thinking connects you with a massive reservoir of thought that tends to replicate its results in your experience.

You can just as easily—actually far *more* easily—tap into the pool of thought generated by healthy people and those who have been healed of that ailment. Access to well-being comes more easily because wellness is more natural than illness. But first you must be a match to wellness in consciousness. You cannot concentrate on darkness and find light. You cannot focus on disease and find healing. You cannot immerse yourself in fear and find love.

Support groups

Many people participate in support groups with others who face the same illness or problem. Such groups can provide meaningful help, as members do not feel alone in their challenge, they find a venue to vent their feelings, and they may receive information and inspiration about how to overcome or deal more masterfully with their situation. Meetings like these can provide comfort and empowerment.

Support groups can also hamper members' progress by emphasizing their identification with the disease, underscoring the limitations the disease represents, and reinforcing a victim mentality. If you attend a support group, ask yourself, "Do I feel stronger and freer as a result of the meeting?" "Am I more identified with the disease, or do I see myself as greater than it?" "Does the group teach me that I will always need it, or does it help me grow beyond it?" These criteria apply not only to support groups, but to religions, therapies, political parties, and coffee cloches. Any gathering that makes you feel smaller is counterproductive. Any meeting that liberates you is a valuable investment of your time and energy.

You may wish to establish your own support group with a handful of friends dedicated to freeing yourselves from limiting labels and beliefs. Make a date with two or three friends to meet regularly in person or via phone or video, with the intention to uplift and empower each other. Choose people who stimulate you with positive vision rather than drag you down with complaints or commiseration. Talk about your goals, visions, and progress. If you bring up a challenge, pivot as quickly as possible to find ways to overcome the issue rather than dwelling on it. Affirm, meditate, pray, and share resources. Such gatherings will become one of your most cherished activities. I have participated in several homemade support groups, and found them to be extremely worthwhile.

You may not have a lot of people in your life with whom you can discuss spiritual or uplifting ideas. You don't need a large congregation or community to establish and sustain healing. One or two trusted friends is enough. Better to have a few good friends who lift you rather than a lot who bring you down. True friends see the best in you and are not fooled by the labels the world assigns you. The only label that fits you is "divine expression of a perfect God."

No one likes to be identified with one limiting aspect of their life. People who make a living being known for their body, or a particular career, or a defining moment in their life, feel a certain gnawing emptiness. A deeper part of them is screaming, "There is more to me than the thing you are focusing on! Please don't shrink me to one attribute!" Any physical, emotional, or mental trait by which you identify a human being falls short of their true self and fails to capture their divine essence. Ultimately everyone you meet is God. Yet even that term is severely limited, tainted by many constricting human ideas. Religious Jews aren't allowed to speak or write the name of God because God cannot be defined. As an expression of God, neither can you be defined. For every label you are given or you accept, there is a greater you that lives beyond it.

In the world we must use labels. But we don't have to get stuck in them. The real you lives far beyond labels. Identify with how God created you, rather than what the world has made of you. At any moment you can peel away the stickers pasted over love, break out of the boxes that have kept you small, and step into the light. Then you will truly be free.

MASTER KEYS *of* THIS CHAPTER

1. The labels you have been given do not define you. The real you lives far beyond any label.

2. You are not your diagnosis. Take care not to identify with any disease.

3. When you say, "I am," be sure to follow that statement with words that describe who you wish to be and, in truth, you are.

4. The best healers do not focus on their patients' histories. They heal in the here and now, and guide their patients to fresh possibilities.

5. Because the world is a dream more than a reality, more liquid than solid, more energy than matter, anything can change to anything at any time, including disease shifting to wellness.

6. When you remove your attention from disease, you shift to the experience of wellness.

7. All "conditions" are temporary and changing. Don't give your power to conditions, for yourself or others.

8. Every time you tell a story, you reinforce it. Take care what stories you tell. You can trade your old story of illness for a new story of wellness.

9. When visioning your ideal life, be sure not to include any elements that are not ideal.

10. Support groups can be helpful as long as they help you rise beyond your difficulty rather than reinforcing it.

IN MY WORLD
ALL IS WELL

Health is a state of body. Wellness is a state of being.

—J. Stanford

Sri Nisargadatta Maharaj was a spiritual master in the Advaita (Oneness of All Life) tradition. He proclaimed, "In my world all is well." What a strange statement for a person to make! Didn't he watch the news? Wasn't he depressed by the starvation and wars that plagued his country, and the appalling poverty on the backstreets of Mumbai? How could he buffer himself from the real world? If Nisargadatta didn't see the horrors of this world, what world did he see? Even more important: If that man can live in a world where all is well, can I live there too? And if so, how can I get there?

A Course in Miracles differentiates between the world God created and the world the ego, or the limited sense of self, made. God's world is comprised of all that is good, eternal, loving, joyful, and soul-rewarding. We call that state "heaven." We don't have to die to get to heaven. We can enter it at any time by choosing thoughts, feelings, and actions aligned with it. The ego's world, by contrast, is built on fear, separation, emptiness, war, and death—the domain that seems inescapable when we equate ourselves with a body and regard the physical world as the only reality. The purpose of our spiritual journey is to depart the false world of fear and return to the real world of love. Nisargadatta said, "Love is seeing the unity under the imaginary diversity."

Disease is an attribute of the ego's world, and healing is an attribute of God's world. God recognizes us as immortal, untarnished spirits. When you love someone, you see the best in them and you want only good for them. You take no delight in their pain, and all delight in their well-being. Get beyond any belief that God finds any purpose in our sorrow or suffering. If we are going to escape a hellish world and enter a heavenly experience, we must see the world as God sees it. When the disciple Peter expressed his doubts to Jesus, the master told him, "You aren't thinking as God thinks. You are thinking as a man thinks." In this crucial feedback we find the answer to the question, "How can I live in a world where all is well?"

Crossing the Bridge

Bruno Gröning, who effected thousands of miraculous healings, forbade his patients to state their diagnoses or talk about their illnesses. Fixating on symptoms, he explained, perpetuates them. Gröning instructed his followers to think, talk, and focus only on wellness and God. Illness, he said, is the result of wrong perception, and it can be corrected by right seeing. To even see illness is a form of wrong thinking. *A Course in Miracles* tells us, "Spiritual vision literally cannot see error." To recognize wholeness in spite of the appearance of illness is the most powerful healing tool. Bruno Gröning called us to give reality only to the good, and let all else go.

After my mother had cataract surgery, she spent a few days in a residential recovery facility. On the center of the patients' dining room table a little card requested, *"Please do not discuss your illness at the table."* Even a medical institution realized that talking about illness is a downer! Bruno Gröning would extrapolate the advisory: "Please do not discuss your illness. Period." You have probably noticed that when one person in a group starts talking about an illness, traffic accident, or disaster, immediately others in the group chime in with their similar stories, and quickly the conversation plummets. Unchecked, negativity is contagious. Misery truly does love company.

If you refuse to give attention to illness and evil, where do they go? Back to the nothingness from which they came. Where does a dream monster go when you wake up? What has no substance does not have to be resisted, attacked, defeated, or stuffed somewhere. The more you fight a dream monster, the more you stay trapped in the nightmare. You might defeat the monster, but you are still dreaming and subject to the whims of dreams. The next monster is just around the corner. Monsters can threaten or defeat you only when you sink into the dimension where they have power. In another reality they do not exist.

In the inspiring documentary, *Fat, Sick, and Nearly Dead,* Joe Cross found himself at the end of his rope, 100 pounds overweight, jammed with steroids, and suffering from an autoimmune disease. One day Joe got fed up with feeling awful and he took charge of his life by fasting on fresh juices. Over time he lost a great deal of weight and became radiantly healthy. Joe placed a juicer in the back of his car and drove across America, inviting over 500 people along the way to enjoy fresh juices and reap their benefits.

At a truck stop Joe met miserably unhealthy 429-pound Phil, trudging through his life consigned to 18 medications; his doctor warned him that he was a cheeseburger away from a heart attack. Joe took Phil under his wing and guided him to embrace a juice diet, on which he lost hundreds of pounds, dumped his medications, and became happy and healthy—a truly miraculous transformation. In a final scene, we see a far lighter and brighter Phil working in a health food store turning customers on to the benefits of juicing.

Sometimes we have to get so sick of a life that isn't working that we reach for one that does. Symptoms get our attention to motivate us to claim wellness instead. Rather than dwelling on symptoms, we can pivot on them. We can use our experience of contrast to make a better choice. "This can't be it!" is the first step to discovering and claiming, "This is it!" Even our symptoms were part of "in my world, all is well" because they lit a fire under us to ascend to a higher rung of wellness.

How to Make Affirmations Work for You

While many people use affirmations to achieve and sustain wellness, they don't fully understand how and why they work. If they did, their affirmations would yield faster, stronger, and deeper results. When you utter an affirmation, you are not convincing yourself of something you want to be true. You are reminding yourself of something that already *is* true.

The mind is composed of three strata: On the surface level the *conscious mind* thinks an endless stream of random thoughts, mostly untrue, instilled largely by fear and cultural programming. Yogis call this "the monkey mind," as it darts about wildly, confused and distracted. This mind must be stilled and transcended to achieve illumination, clarity, and inner peace.

Below the conscious mind, the *subconscious mind* is the repository of the feelings, beliefs, and attitudes we are unwilling or unable to hold in our conscious mind. They are emotion-fueled, the repository of past pleasures we filed in our memory bank so we can repeat them, or past pain we wish to avoid repeating. Undoing erroneous beliefs in our subconscious is crucial to our healing because the subconscious determines our experience far more than the conscious mind. I heard about a woman who was not recovering from a relatively minor surgical operation. After a few weeks, a psychologist hypnotized the patient to try to access her subconscious beliefs. During hypnosis she recalled that while she was asleep under anesthesia, she heard the surgeon say, "I doubt that she will recover." The psychologist then interviewed the surgeon, who admitted he had made that statement—but it was about another patient he and the surgical team were discussing. Yet the patient, unaware of that element of the conversation, assumed the statement applied to her, and her subconscious played out the dire prognosis that had nothing to do with her. Given the truth about the situation, she soon recovered.

Freud was correct in likening the mind to an iceberg with a small portion showing above the water surface and the far greater volume below. The key to improving your health, finances, and relationships is to upgrade your subconscious beliefs. To achieve this: (1) Formulate and practice affirmations that edify the beliefs you prefer to manifest; (2) Mobilize prayer to ask Higher Power to do what you cannot consciously do, and heal you or a circumstance; (3) Pay significant attention to people, words, images, and experiences that match your desired situation.

Below the subconscious mind sits the *superconscious mind*. Psychology teachers usually erroneously depict the superconscious as above the conscious, floating in space like the blue sky a child draws as a thin strip at the top of a finger painting. Yet the superconscious is not somewhere outside of us; it is imbedded deep *within* us at the core of our being. The superconscious is your memory bank of truth. It is literally the mind of God, seeded indelibly within you. A part of you knows all that God knows. You may forget the truth, ignore or deny it, but universal wisdom remains hard-coded into you. No person or experience can undo it. What God knows in you is absolutely, unequivocally, indelibly, eternally so.

When you practice an affirmation, you are sending a pipeline from your conscious mind through your subconscious into your superconscious, like a drill penetrates the earth until it reaches a pure, natural reservoir of water. When you tap into that pool of wisdom, you can draw its healing contents to the surface and make practical use of the precious resource. One of the best descriptions I have heard about how an affirmation works is, *"The spirit within me loves to hear the truth about itself."* When you do an affirmation properly, you feel uplifted, empowered, and healed. You have achieved resonance with the mind and heart of God. Nothing is more edifying than remembering that you are whole and loveable, you deserve the best that the universe has to offer, and you can mobilize the magnificent principles that make life work.

Here are some examples of affirmations that will lift and heal you:

All is well.

Life is good, and I am good in it.

I am whole, healthy, and happy.

I am loved, guided, cared for, protected, and safe.

All things are working together for good.

God's timing is perfect.

I love as God loves,
and I reap the infinite blessings that love bestows.

> Every dollar I spend enriches the economy,
> blesses everyone it touches,
> and returns to me multiplied.
>
> My mind is receptive, my heart is wide open,
> and miracles unfold before me.
>
> I know who I am and what I am here to do.
>
> I am perfect as God created me.

You don't have to say an affirmation a thousand times, although if you enjoy doing so, you certainly can. A few slow, deliberate, sincere repetitions can take you where you need to go. When you get the sense that you have accessed a deeper truth that feels right and real to you, you are there. Because we are spiritual beings, it is the *quality of experience* that makes our life worthwhile. When you gain the experience the affirmation is intended to generate, you and the affirmation have succeeded.

Feel free to formulate your own affirmations. You will be guided. You can also turn to spiritual teachers who have meditated on affirmations and passed them along to you. Louise L. Hay has done landmark work in formulating affirmations that offset specific illnesses. Her classic books *Heal Your Body* and *You Can Heal Your Life* are marvelous repositories of guidance and inspiration. No matter what route you take, one thing is for sure: When you remind yourself of what is true, something inside you stirs and that truth becomes established in your experience.

Proper Use of Denials

Over the past few decades, "denial" has become a dirty word in psychology, self-help, and recovery circles. We regularly hear, "You are in denial about your problem." This notion is well-founded in that many of us are asleep to habits that are hurting us, and we need to bring those patterns to our awareness so we can replace them with behaviors that serve us better.

There is a metaphysical application of denial that is positive, powerful, and practical. Just as affirmations validate truths that help us, denials offset illusions that hurt us. The first step to reveal a truth is to peel away the lies that cover it. To know yourself as an expansive spiritual being, you must deny that you are a limited physical being. To attract a healthy, available partner, you must deny the belief that "all the good ones are taken or they're gay." To allow more money into your life, you must dissolve the thought that money is the root of all evil. An endless parade of false beliefs keeps the world spinning in small, tight, confining circles. If we are going to escape the prison of limiting beliefs, we must boldly, flatly, and overtly deny the "realities" those beliefs have created, and replace them with realities that work far better.

Here are some denials that will lead you to higher ground:

I am not subject to the economy to which most people subscribe. God is the source of my supply.

Politics have no power over my life.
I dwell in the sovereign state of my own consciousness.

Fear is the liar.
Love is the truth.

No person has the ability to make me happy or unhappy.
My happiness depends on me.

My job is not the source of my wealth.
My job is but one channel among an infinite number of
avenues through which abundance can reach me.

From *A Course in Miracles*:

I am not a body. I am free. I am as God created me.

There is no death.
The Son of God [my own true self] is free.

I am under no laws but God's.

You will notice that most of the denials are followed by
an affirmation. That's because we need to replace the false
belief with a positive alternative. The subconscious does not
hear "no." When it hears "no death," the word it registers
is "death." So we need to follow the denial of death with
an affirmation of life. The denial works with the conscious
mind that understands "no," while the affirmation works
with the subconscious mind that is built on the positive
images it is fed.

Where to Place Your Faith

To accept and live in a world of wellness requires a leap
of faith. This is not a leap *to* faith, but more a *transfer* of faith.
While many people claim they have no faith, we all live by
faith in many people and things. When you drive across
a bridge, you have faith that the structure will stay intact
until you reach the other side. When you eat at a restaurant,
you have faith that the chef used ingredients that will not
poison you. The restaurant has faith that you will pay after
you eat. When you walk across a street at a green light, you
have faith that cars will stop at the red light until you finish

crossing. All of our lives are built on deep faith in countless people, principles, and processes. To say that you don't have faith is a spectacular delusion. We all live by constant faith.

The question is not whether you have faith, but whether your faith is *well-placed* or *misplaced*. We either invest our faith in illusions that leave us sad and empty, or in truth that nourishes and empowers us. You can tell whether or not you have invested your faith wisely by the results you experience. Misery indicates that you have placed your trust in false beliefs. Soul reward demonstrates that you trust what is real. The world you live in demonstrates where you have placed your faith.

When Pontius Pilate asked Jesus, "Are you the king of the Jews?" Jesus brilliantly answered, "My kingdom is not of this world." His faith was not in national politics or divisive religion, but in a dimension that transcends personality preferences, dogmatic differences, and petty squabbles. You and I have equal access to that dimension. Jesus and other spiritual masters do not have a secret key to the kingdom of heaven; they have plainly given us the keys to join them there.

Sri Nisargadatta did not say, "In my world, some things are well." He said, "All is well." In that simple statement he was urging us not to settle for less than total fulfillment. This sounds crazy in a world built on compromise, but it is compromise that is crazy. We must withdraw our allegiance to a world built on suffering and take refuge in a world built on wellness. When you refuse to accept illusions, you reclaim the wholeness you knew before you were convinced you were broken. Then you can say with full confidence, like the spiritual master, "In my world, all is well."

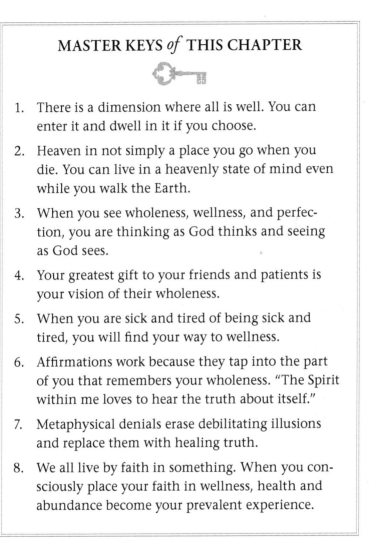

MASTER KEYS *of* THIS CHAPTER

1. There is a dimension where all is well. You can enter it and dwell in it if you choose.

2. Heaven in not simply a place you go when you die. You can live in a heavenly state of mind even while you walk the Earth.

3. When you see wholeness, wellness, and perfection, you are thinking as God thinks and seeing as God sees.

4. Your greatest gift to your friends and patients is your vision of their wholeness.

5. When you are sick and tired of being sick and tired, you will find your way to wellness.

6. Affirmations work because they tap into the part of you that remembers your wholeness. "The Spirit within me loves to hear the truth about itself."

7. Metaphysical denials erase debilitating illusions and replace them with healing truth.

8. We all live by faith in something. When you consciously place your faith in wellness, health and abundance become your prevalent experience.

HOW
HEALING
HAPPENS

PERMISSION SLIPS

*The art of medicine consists of amusing
the patient while nature cures the disease.*

—Voltaire

In rural West Bengal, India, many people believe that if they are bitten by a dog, they have become pregnant with the dog's puppies. Bite victims rush to a local witch doctor, who gives them yogurt and herbs and tells them that they are no longer pregnant. Then they go home relieved.

From a medical and scientific viewpoint, such a belief is ridiculous. Yet this process illustrates a dynamic that affects healing far beyond West Bengal. Belief plays a far greater factor in illness and healing than most people realize. We think ourselves sick and we think ourselves well. It is not so much the doctor or medicine that heals us, but our faith in that person or method. You will get healed by who and what you believe in. More fundamentally, you will get healed by your choice to be healed.

A Course in Miracles tells us that the real physician is the mind of the patient. Patients choose healers who play out their intentions. The physician, the Course tells us, is not needed at all. The patient could just decide, "I have no use for this illness," rise up, and be healed. The Course also tells us that every sickness could be healed immediately.

Healers, then, are permission slips by which patients give themselves permission to heal, or not. If you intend to get healed, you will find a doctor who will heal you. If you choose not to be healed, you will find a doctor, or many, who will not heal you. The choice for illness and healing lies squarely in the hands of the patient.

This dynamic flies in the face of what we have been taught about how sickness and healing occur. We have been taught that we are subject to all kinds of adverse influences that can rob us of health and life. Then we choose from a spectrum of healers to offset the ailment. In both cases we are disempowered, as we ascribe our ill health to external influences, and then we give our power to external agents to remove them. This is the inverse of how health works. We are the creators of our experience and the masters of our lives. We are not passive recipients of the effects of a chaotic, impersonal, whimsical universe. Mind is cause, and the physical world is effect. We participate in everything that happens to us by virtue of the beliefs we hold and the feelings we entertain. Our mind and intentions source the world we see; we are not victims, but creators. *A Course in Miracles* urges us to remember:

I am responsible for what I see.

I choose the feelings I experience,
and I decide upon the goal I would achieve.

And everything that seems to happen to me I ask for,
and receive as I have asked.

The ego does not want to hear such a radical statement of responsibility. It regards itself as the effect of other people's choices and uncontrollable external influences. But the only true influence is mind. This is where your power lies, and the only place where you will gain mastery of your life. When you accept one hundred percent responsibility for the experience you have created, you gain one hundred percent of the power to create the experiences you now prefer. That is how powerful you are, and the authority with which Higher Power has entrusted you.

All Healing is Faith Healing

Cross-cultural studies show that healers of all kinds obtain similar rates of success with their patients. Medical doctors, acupuncturists, chiropractors, naturopaths, homeopaths, herbalists, energy workers, shamans, faith healers, and witch doctors are all equally effective with the patients who believe in them. As Jesus told a woman who was healed in his presence, "Your faith has made you whole."

Go to the healer or participate in the healing regime you believe in. The healer you have faith in will help you. If you go to a physician or use a method you don't believe in, your efforts will be for naught. You will waste time and money, and perhaps get sicker. Don't be distracted by methods that others tell you will work, but do not work for you. Seek instead what resonates with you, and move in that direction. Then you will be in alignment with your beliefs, and maximize your ability to get well.

By the same token, never attempt to heal someone who does not believe in you or your method. Your patient will not be healed by *your* beliefs; they will be healed by *their* beliefs. My client Dr. Brand, a medical doctor, struggled with a patient who was not following his directions, and not improving. During one of her appointments, the patient told the doctor she heard about an acupuncturist she thought could help her. Dr. Brand resisted her idea because he wanted to be the physician who healed her and he believed his system was better. In coaching with me he realized that he was stuck on his method and he sincerely wanted the patient to heal. He came up with this statement to her: "I am committed to your healing, happiness, and well-being. If you can find that through my treatment, I would be very pleased. If you can find that elsewhere, I support you to head in that direction. *How* you get healed is less important that *that* you get healed." Dr. Brand sighed with relief as he found the place inside himself that genuinely championed his patient's success. The patient later told him that she saw the acupuncturist, and felt better. I encouraged my client not to take this result personally; it was more about the patient's belief than his skill. Many other patients were well satisfied with his treatments. Ego says, "Healing has to happen *my* way." Spirit says, "Any way that healing comes is a blessing."

Permission to Not Heal

Some clients use a healer as a permission slip to *not* heal. The client's intention to hold onto a sickness or problem is stronger than his intention to release it, so the issue lingers. Yet even in cases where the patient does not heal, the healer serves.

Consider a patient who has gotten divorced and harbors deep-seated guilt, anger, or resentment that he is unwilling to let go. He may experience physical symptoms fueled by his emotional turmoil. Over time the patient consults one or many healers, without improvement. He keeps banging his head against the wall, not realizing that in order to heal he must release his resistance. Let's say this patient needs to get frustrated over a series of twenty unsuccessful healing treatments with one or several healers, before he is willing to reconsider his position and quit badgering himself. Let's also say you are healer number twelve in the progression toward his ultimate awakening. Even though the patient did not exhibit healing as a result of your interaction, you helped him by allowing him to practice resistance on you and progress toward learning that it is not serving him. Through your interaction he has advanced toward his eventual choice for healing.

It would be nice if you could wave a magic wand and take away your client's pain or problem. But the client must be willing to choose healing. You cannot choose for him. One day he will get there. A teacher I know conducted a weekend seminar in which one participant was hostile. He cursed the teacher out and left the program. Eight years later the teacher received an email from the student apologizing for his rude behavior. He had been going through a tough time he did not know how to resolve, so he took out his upset on the teacher and the seminar. Over the years he grew to understand his process and he found his way to peace. So that seminar, although apparently a failure for that participant, served as a template upon which he practiced his self-defeating behavior, which eventually led him to recognize it didn't work, and then grow beyond it.

A client's path to healing may take many twists and turns that make no sense to the reasoning mind, but end up leading the person to the mountaintop. If you were a tennis instructor and your student made a number of bad serves in your presence, you would not consider yourself a failure. The client had to learn from bad serves before he could achieve good ones. We learn from our mistakes as well as our successes. "The record books never show the score at halftime." While we tend to be fixated on the end goal, what the patient learns en route to the goal is the real gold.

The Source of All Healing

Ultimately your healing relationship is not with a person or a technique. It is with the Source of all life. All that you need to be healed is within you and available to you. God did not cast us into a cruel universe where we lack what we need and must search for it endlessly. The quest for healing ends within.

Genuine healers give credit to Higher Power as the source of their patients' transformation. Then the practitioner through whom healing is delivered is free of the karma of identifying as a healer. She accepts neither credit nor blame. She is a player in the movie for which the patient has written the script. The healer is happy to serve in this capacity.

Doctors are not the source of healing because they cannot heal themselves. If doctors possessed the power to heal, they would not get sick and they would live forever. But doctors get sick and die like everyone else. Doctors treat; life force heals. If you worship a doctor, you have delivered your gift to the wrong altar. Thank and reward doctors for their brilliant, helpful, compassionate, life-saving service. They are blessings to the world. I am deeply grateful to the doctors who have helped me. Just don't attribute healing power to persons. They are channels through which the Source of all wellness flows. They did not make up the rules of healing; they are cooperating with them.

If someone asked you, "Where does your drinking water come from?" you might answer, "From the faucet in the kitchen." And that would be correct. Yet that faucet is but the final point of delivery in a far vaster system. The faucet receives its water from your home's water tank. Before that, it goes through a long series of pipes proceeding from a reservoir. The reservoir is filled by water that cascades from the mountains. The mountains collect water from rain and snow, which falls from clouds in the sky. The clouds formed from evaporated sea or other water. The system by which water comes to you is far, far, far greater than the last gate through which it passes. And who created the bigger system? Ultimately all water, like all sustenance, comes from the Grace of God.

Use permission slips as long as you need them. Be a permission slip to others as long as they need you and you choose to be used as such. If you are not ready to accept healing directly from the universe, let the universe help you through a person or method. We serve in our highest capacity as channels for healing. One day we will grow beyond faith in forms and our faith will be established only in Spirit. Thank God for people who help, and thank God for being the Source of that help. We are forever held mercifully and gracefully in the hands of God.

MASTER KEYS *of* THIS CHAPTER

1. All healers, tools, techniques, and rituals serve as permission slips for patients to achieve their intention to be healed.

2. If a client chooses not to be healed, he or she will use a permission slip to generate that result.

3. We are each responsible for our experience. External factors do not cause our lives; we cause them by the internal choices we make.

4. All healing is faith healing. You get healed because you have faith in your practitioner or method. Many kinds of different practitioners achieve equally valid results because their patients believe in them and their techniques.

5. Do not attempt to heal someone who does not believe in you or your method. That person is either not ready to be healed, or they are better matched with a different healer or method.

6. Even if you cannot heal a patient, you contribute to that patient's healing by providing an experience that advances that patient's learning curve that will eventually lead them to the choice for healing.

7. The real healer is God. All good doctors and healers serve as vehicles through which Life Force heals.

DON'T RATION
YOUR PASSION

A merry heart doeth good like a medicine,
but a broken spirit dries the bones.

— PROVERBS 17:22

Morton Lauridsen is a genius musician considered by many to be one of the world's greatest living composers of choral music. He is widely respected for his stirring opus, "Lux Aeterna" ("Eternal Light"). Morton recounts that one of his dear friends, a conductor who often conducts Lauridsen's compositions, fell into a coma. After several weeks, doctors could not predict whether or not the man would awaken.

Morton went to see his friend, lying inert in a hospital bed. After a few minutes Morton began to softly sing the chorus of "Lux Aeterna." Then, to onlookers' astonishment, the patient raised his hand as if he were conducting a chorus. This was the first time the man displayed any activity since he had fallen comatose. Eventually he regained full waking consciousness. (For a moving journey into Lauridsen's exalted music, watch the documentary *Shining Night,* available at innerharmony.com.)

While some people decry passion as a tool of the devil, properly directed it is a tool of God. Passion is life's way of moving you to be in your right place at the right time with the right people for the right purpose. When you feel passionate about something, the universe is encouraging you to move in that direction for the betterment of your life and the lives you touch.

If you feel ill or tired, or you know someone who is, answering three key questions can pave the way to restore energy and health:

What do you feel most passionate about?

Are you expressing that passion fully?

If not, what would you need to do
to creatively express that passion?

This simple formula works when (1) you are honest about where your passion lives and what it would take to bring it forth; and (2) you find the courage to put those changes into action.

While Morton Lauridsen's friend was medically comatose, many people are spiritually comatose. Even while we walk, talk, eat, go to work, and execute our daily activities, we are engulfed in a dream of smallness, forgetting who we are and why we are here. In the poignant film *Joe Versus the Volcano,* Meg Ryan's character sums up our predicament and its antidote: "Almost the whole world is asleep. Everybody you know. Everybody you see. Everybody you talk to. Only a few people are awake, and they live in a state of constant total amazement."

Passion Places Everyone in their Perfect Position

Just out of college I took a job working in a sheltered workshop for people with severe mental disabilities. I was not interested in that kind of work, but I needed the money. While I enjoyed my relationships with the clients, for the most part I found the job a drudgery. It wasn't long before I was coming to work late and making excuses to get out of the facility. Then I developed physical symptoms of illness, but I had to stay in the job for 60 days to get the medical benefits to address the symptoms from staying in the job. Meanwhile I was yearning for a career more aligned with my passion—writing, teaching, and playing music. But I did not want to be a quitter, so I hung in there. As time went on, I found myself in a deeper and deeper rut, until I realized that to maintain my psychological and physical health I had to leave. The moment I gave my notice, I felt free. My symptoms disappeared and I started to feel good again. That was the turning point when I began to write and teach, the activities that have blossomed into a lifetime career that has fulfilled me in the most important ways and supported many others on their spiritual journeys.

A month after I quit the job, I went back to visit the facility. There I met the fellow who had replaced me. Immediately I realized that he was infinitely better suited for the job than I was. He loved being there, he was extremely effective with the clients, and I later learned that he enjoyed far more longevity at the place than I did. He was the perfect person for that job. While I had denied my passion by being in a place I didn't belong, and allowed guilt to keep me there, I was stealing that man's right job from him, and the perfect supervisor for the clients. When I finally trusted my guidance and followed it, everything lined up for all of us to be in our right places.

We get sick because we live in sickening ways. We stay in jobs, relationships, and living situations that drag us down and deplete our life force. Illness is an indication that you have worn your batteries down beyond a crucial point. But you don't have to get sick to get the message and change. You have a brilliant inner guide that will keep you from getting to that point, and rescue you if you do. Your voice of passion is your guide to health. When you do what you love, your body secretes all kinds of amazing hormones and chemicals like oxytocin, dopamine, serotonin, and endorphins, which keep you happy and healthy. You don't need to go searching the outer world for feel-good drugs. When you live true to your joy, your body will provide you with the natural chemistry you need to get and stay high.

Eliminating the things you love is not wellness.
Wellness feeds your soul and makes you feel good.

—IMAN

A Day Worth Living

At the end of each day ask yourself, "In what moments today was I really alive, with my heart open, feeling grateful, and expressing myself joyfully?" You may be shocked, as I sometimes am, to realize that there were just a few moments during your day, if that, when you were fully present and passionate. Those moments are the clues to how you were born to live and what you are here to do. They are arrows pointing you home. Don't write off the soul-stirring moments as anomalies to your life. Boredom, frustration, and a sense of purposelessness are the anomalies. Life was not meant to be sea of troubles with a few shining moments. The shining moments are the keys to your mission and your destiny.

Rather than trudging through your obligations and waiting to wedge passion-filled moments in the few cracks left over, make it your first priority to act on your inspiration.

Set passionate activities into your schedule and give them precedence over rote tasks. One of my greatest joys is writing, so I start my day with it. I go to a distraction-free area on my property and I dive into my creative writing for several hours, which proves to be one of the most rewarding times of my day. Then I go to my office and do emails, phone calls, and other necessary tasks. After I have finished my writing stint, I feel that my day is worthwhile; if nothing else interesting happens, that time was well spent.

On a broader scale, don't wait weeks, months, or years to schedule activities that bring you joy. Build dinners and visits with friends, massages, concerts, weekend getaways, uplifting seminars, immersion in nature, and vacations into your schedule *before* work and obligations encroach on your schedule and you have no space for soul renewal. It's very easy for "shoulds" to fill up your time so you have none left over for "woulds." You must choose self-nurturing activities for yourself; no one is going to sweep you away from your desk and take you on a cruise. If you don't honor your passion, it won't get honored. You *can* choose in favor of joy, and you will.

Have You Recited Lately?

A poet went to a doctor and complained of all kinds of annoying symptoms. The doctor examined the fellow and asked him, "When was the last time you recited your poetry?"

The poet thought for a moment and answered, "Several months ago."

"Then please recite your favorite new poem for me," the doctor requested.

The patient arose and gave a stirring recitation. The doctor repeated the request and the patient recited several more poems.

"How do you feel now?" asked the doctor.

"I feel wonderful!" he exuded.

"Good," the doctor responded. "Denying your talent and passion made you ill. Now go home and keep creating and you will stay well."

Your body and your life are always giving you feedback as to how much or little you are attuned with your passion and expressing it. Energy, creativity, and a sense of well-being are signs that you are on track with your soul's purpose. Numbness, fatigue, and depression are signs that you are stifling your true self. Authentic self-expression is the great antidote to stress-related maladies, as it provides a positive outlet for energy literally aching to flow. The ache is a sign that the river of life wants to move through you. When you allow it, healing and miracles occur.

High Involvement, Low Attachment

Your job is to tap into your passion and express it. Where it ends up is not your business. This principle is called "high involvement, low attachment." You may have an idea about where your acting, art project, book, or business plan is supposed to land. Sometimes you are correct; often you are not. Giving your gift is more important than managing its results.

After my novel *Linden's Last Life* was published, I wrote a screenplay for it. I visioned that this metaphysical adventure would capture the hearts and imagination of lots of people and bestow them with a profound inspiring message. I shopped the screenplay to a number of agents and studios. Some told me they were very impressed; one high-level producer enrolled a well-known actor to play the lead, but the project didn't come to fruition. After a bunch of efforts, no one picked up the screenplay. I was disappointed.

During a coaching session with Bashar, I asked him why the movie did not materialize as I had anticipated.

"Did you enjoy writing the screenplay?" he asked.

"Very much."

"Was it a passionate, creative, rewarding process for you?"

"Absolutely."

"Then it was a success," Bashar explained. "Expressing your passion is fulfilling unto itself. Where it goes after that is up to the universe. Don't try to boss the outcome. Do it because you love to do it. That is reason enough."

When Bashar said that, something clicked for me. I was fully alive in writing the screenplay; every moment of that process was healing and enlivening, and sent out ripples of well-being into the universe. It would have been exciting to see the screenplay produced, just as it would be for your meaningful project to come to fruition. Our projects may indeed manifest. In the meantime, spiritual reward is even more important than material fruition. If your project is to take form and reach the masses, it will. If you are to participate in how that happens, you will be shown your role. Meanwhile, your experience of creating is as important as the physical product. The physical project is the point of attention that stimulates and focalizes the generation of positive energy, which is life-giving to you and those you touch with your talent. From a higher perspective, your energy *is* your product and service.

When Dee and I lived in Fiji, we became close with a native family who cared for our property. One day we gave the children some colorful t-shirts we had bought for them. A few days later we saw some kids in the local village wearing those t-shirts. The family had given them away. Dee and I laughed and realized that we could not be attached to what our friends did with their gifts. Our job was to give with a whole heart. After that, the t-shirts were in God's hands. If God wanted those t-shirts to go to the village kids, that was fine with us.

I love the motto, "launch and release." I saw an interview with the Director of Mission Control for SpaceX, after the successful launch of a rocket. He humbly stated, "'Mission control' is an illusion. Once you launch the rocket, there is very little you can do to control it. You just have to watch where it goes and hope it ends up where you intended."

Trust that your expressions will find their right place in the universe. Maybe the kids in the village needed the t-shirts more than the family we gave them to. Maybe the joy Dee and I experienced in giving those t-shirts was the real gift to us and the recipients. Maybe the universe has clever ways to deliver your project to all the right people who can benefit from it, and who will in turn reward you. In the meantime, the aliveness you feel in creating will heal you more than struggling to force a pre-set result. It's wonderful when your efforts achieve a desired goal. But the joy of the journey is more important than a particular trophy you might receive. The process is as important as the product. The goals you reach for are life's way of enticing you to take an exhilarating ride. As Jewish theologian Martin Buber stated, "All journeys have destinations of which the traveler is unaware."

When you stay true to your passion, life takes on color, meaning, and purpose. To stifle your passion is to deny God's will for you. To express it is to allow God to touch the world. The relationship between passionate self-expression and vibrant health is unrefutable. A composer got a conductor to come out of a coma when doctors couldn't. Now the baton is in your hand. It's time to raise your arm and give a concert that moves the world, beginning with your own.

MASTER KEYS *of* THIS CHAPTER

1. Passion is the universe's way of guiding you to be in your right place at the right time with the right people for the right purpose.

2. When you live true to your passion, you achieve maximal results and empower those around you to achieve their maximal results.

3. When you do not follow your passion, you experience emptiness, boredom, frustration, depression, irritability, and possibly illness.

4. Illness is a sign that you have worn your spiritual batteries down. It is a call for you to tell more truth about where your joy lives, and express it.

5. At the end of each day, consider in what moments you lived true to your passion, and in what moments you denied it.

6. Find ways to do more of what you love and less of what depletes your life force.

7. Creative self-expression is healing to the body and soul.

8. The process of self-expression is more important than the results that come of it. Do not be attached to outcomes. Launch your creations and let God arrange their results.

HOW MUCH
HEALING COSTS

God heals and the doctor takes the fees.

—BENJAMIN FRANKLIN

Paul is a yard maintenance man who has two children disabled due to a genetic abnormality. Their condition is lightened by a rare drug that costs $60,000 per month per child. Fortunately, Paul's family has government insurance that covers this astronomical cost. The down side of this coverage is that he must show a low income in order to qualify. So Paul cannot hold any substantial job; he must take odd jobs and get paid what he can off the books. He also has a wife and another child to support.

Do people really need to pay so much for health care? Did God set up the universe so that only the wealthy can receive proper medical attention? Do governments need to pay high medical fees to take care of their citizens? When I went to pick up a prescription at a pharmacy, the clerk asked me, "Do you have insurance for pharmaceuticals?" When I told her, "No, I don't," she did some calculations on her cash register. "That will be fifteen dollars," she told me. After I paid her, I asked, curious, "How much would that prescription cost if I had insurance?" She checked her computer again and replied, "one hundred twenty-five."

Certain facts of life, we have been told, are inescapable: People get sick. Health care is expensive. There is a shortage of qualified, available practitioners. You may have to travel a far distance to obtain the services of a good healer. We need to take drugs and medical treatments that have damaging side effects. But, as the beloved Don Quixote told his sidekick, "Facts, my dear Sancho, are the enemies of truth." There comes a point in every soul's evolution when you withdraw your faith in facts and you become passionate about the truth. Illusions lose their grip and give way to reality. There are deeper truths about what healing costs than we have been led to believe. In this chapter we will shine the light on misconceptions about what you must pay to get healed, and reveal the truths they conceal.

Healing Doesn't Cost

Genuine healing is free. You are not required to pay for well-being or sacrifice anything for it. Health is your birthright, your natural condition, established and sustained by God. No one can give you health, withhold it from you, reserve it for certain privileged people, or charge you for it. Get over any idea that your well-being is in someone else's hands. Your health is entirely a joint venture between you and your Creator.

The purest and most successful healers I know dispense their services freely to all. My mentor Hilda Charlton never charged a penny for the countless healings she performed. Neither did Jesus Christ. Bruno Gröning had no fee. Many humanitarians, including generous doctors, go into impoverished areas and help many people at no charge. The hearts of such practitioners are turned to kindness more than profit. Yet they profit hugely by finding joy that money cannot provide. All of the spiritual healers I mentioned have had all their needs met by people who voluntarily donated to support them, and they wanted for nothing. While such a healing practice requires great faith, it serves as a model of how authentic service blesses both physicians and patients.

Meanwhile, we live in a world where money is a medium of exchange for goods and services. Doctors and other practitioners have their own bills to pay and families to support. They deserve to be rewarded and sustained for the help they deliver. How, then, can we reconcile the truth that God does not charge for healing, while in this world nearly every healing treatment has a cost?

To answer that question, we must zoom the camera of awareness back to the greater picture of how healing works. Begin by recognizing that you have a direct connection with the Source of all life. If you live and breathe, life is living and breathing through you. You can potentially live a healthy life without ever seeing a doctor, taking a pill, or having a surgery. I met a native Hawaiian fellow who told me that his grandmother had just passed away at the age of 117. She lived in a remote village in a very pristine area on Maui. During her lifetime, grandma never rode in a car, watched television, or went to a doctor. We can extract a fundamental clue to good health in this fellow's account: When we stay close to nature and organic ways of living, health follows naturally. The classic 1607 medical text *Regimen Sanitatis Salernitanum,* also known as *Flos Medicinae,* or "The Flower of Medicine," advised, "Use three physicians still: first, Dr. Quiet. Next, Dr. Merryman, and Dr. Dyet." In modern terms: "Let these be your primary doctors: A joyful mind, rest, and a healthy diet."

When you pay a doctor or therapist for their services, you are not paying for healing. You are paying the practitioner for his or her time, skill, treatment, and advice to get

you out of pain. Getting out of pain is not the same as healing. Real healing is a state of mind that manifests in a well
body. When you pay a doctor, you are saying thank you for
your care to relieve my physical distress, and in turn I wish
to support you so you can have your needs met. I gladly pay
doctors for their services, and people gladly pay me for the
services I render. This cycle is called "Happy Money." You
helped me, and now I want to help you.

Genuine healers do not turn away people who cannot
pay. While I charge for my books and programs, I offer many
free services so that people can learn from me at no cost.
In some cases I offer scholarships or tuition discounts. I
donate books to people who don't have the means to pay
for them. The material facts of a healing relationship are
less important than the intention behind it. When you work
with a healer who has a pure intention, you feel welcome,
loved, and cared for. Money is a side issue. If money changes
hands, it is based on appreciation and mutual support. Seek
practitioners who genuinely care about helping you, and the
money piece will take care of itself.

Undoing Erroneous Beliefs about the Cost of Healing

Many of us have been trained to believe and live
out self-defeating ideas about getting or staying healthy.
For example:

> *My health and happiness depend on*
> *people, drugs, and institutions.*
>
> *Healing costs a lot.*
>
> *Nothing good comes for free.*
>
> *I must sacrifice to get what I want.*

The more I pay, the more I receive for what I pay.

My loss is someone else's gain.

No pain, no gain.

If any of these themes occupy real estate in your mind, you must question, test, and challenge them. Are you open to consider that loss buys you nothing, and God does not charge for well-being? This is a book about radical healing; radical because it finds healing in entirely different places than the world tells you it exists. It posits that healing is within your hands, not those of others; that kindness to self gets you more mileage than self-punishment; that you are not required to suffer to find happiness; that money has nothing to do with healing; that your well-being contributes more to the world than your struggle; that you achieve health by allowing it rather than fighting against an alien force. Fighting for health is like waging war to establish peace. You just can't get there from here. The road to peace *is* peace. Well-being is the path as well as the goal.

Healing without Sacrifice

A Course in Miracles tells us that, contrary to what we have been taught, no sacrifice, loss, or payment is required to receive healing. The only "sacrifice" we need make, the Course suggests, is fear, the root of all sorrows. Healing is not about trading something good for something better. It is about trading what is worthless for what is worthwhile; what has no meaning for what has all meaning; replacing self-defeating thoughts with empowering ones; letting go of fear and claiming love.

When I visited the temple of Palenque in Mexico, the tour guide explained that during the time of the ancients, when there was little rain, the priests made human sacrifices to appease the gods. The longer the drought went on, the more lives were taken. When the drought finally ended and rain came, the priests concluded that the volume of murder had finally satisfied the gods. A modern intelligent mind recognizes the tragedy of such a belief and practice. The deaths of many people did not cause rain. It would have come anyway. Prayers without killing would have accomplished the same. While we may call such a belief system primitive, to this day we believe that the more I give up money or other things I value, the faster healing will come. Healing comes not because of money or sacrifice. Healing comes by virtue of grace and a change of mind.

What helps you doesn't have to hurt you. My coaching client Deb has been taking several medications, including an anti-depressant. "The problem is, for every issue the medications alleviate, they create two other problems, some of which are really nasty," she explained. I asked Deb if she was open to believing that she could be helped without sustaining an equal or greater loss. "Can you imagine a cure that fixes what's wrong without requiring more fixes?" Deb's dilemma seemed to be about the medications she was taking, but on a deeper level she was being called to examine her belief that winning in one way requires losing in another. We then began to explore alternatives to her medication that would not require pain. Eventually she found her way to a naturopathic physician who helped her overcome her depression, with the aid of natural supplements that did not cause negative side effects. Wellness does not include elements unlike itself.

When Profit Distracts

Dee and I used to take our dogs to a veterinarian who had a holistic approach, and got wonderful results with our fur babies. Occasionally this vet was absent and she had an associate veterinarian substitute. When the substitute treated our dogs, I was astounded at the very high bills we received, mostly for a variety of tests the primary vet rarely used. Later I learned from a veterinary assistant who quit the clinic, that the associate vet was paid on a commission system; she had a quota of income she was required to produce in order for her to keep her job and get paid.

At one time a lot of my friends used to see a chiropractor they recommended. I was feeling pretty good, but decided to check him out. After my examination he handed me a paper indicating that I needed a treatment plan requiring 28 visits. "Am I that messed up?" I wondered. When I compared notes with my friends, I found that every one of them needed a treatment plan of 28 visits. While I imagine that some of them may have required that regimen, I found it hard to believe that every patient who walked into that office required 28 healing sessions. It is tempting for a healing practitioner to set patients up to be dependent on him. As long as someone benefits from your illness rather than your healing, there is the potential for financial exploitation. Use discernment when working with any healer. While most are ethical, some are not. Among those who are not, many are not even aware that their integrity is out of order. In such a case you must use *your* integrity to substitute for the lack of theirs.

When the coronavirus pandemic hit, a hospital in the southwest geared up to treat lots of Covid-19 patients. As it turned out, because the area is sparsely populated, there were very few Covid-19 cases. The state also prohibited people from coming to the hospital for elective surgeries. As a result, the hospital was relatively empty. After a while it was losing money, so when the no-elective-surgery restriction was lifted, the hospital engaged in a campaign to get people to come to the hospital to be treated. Hospitals and the medical profession are businesses. They depend on people being sick in order to thrive. Hospitals deserve to be paid well for the valuable and life-saving services they deliver; kind, skilled, caring hospital staff members have helped me in ways for which I will always be deeply grateful. Good hospital services are a blessing to humanity. But when hospitals have to start campaigning for patients, we have to question the motive and the system. Medical professionals and institutions should be paid for getting you out of pain, not creating, reinforcing, or maintaining it.

We cannot blame unethical doctors or pharmaceutical companies for overcharging. Your belief system is as much a factor as theirs. As long as you believe you must pay vast amounts for your well-being, you will charge yourself. If you believe that the more you pay, the healthier you will be, you will pay a lot and possibly get healthy. Not because that's the way things are. Because that's the way you believe. You could pay a modest amount, or little, or nothing, and achieve the same results. The world is not the way it is. The world is the way we believe it is.

From Cost to Investment

We can upgrade our understanding about paying for medical services by thinking of health not as having a cost, but requiring an investment. While we usually think of an investment as financial, a more fundamental investment is energetic. This becomes clear when we recognize that money cannot buy health. If it could, the wealthiest people in the world would not get sick or die. But they do. There has to be some other way we can take charge of disease rather than buying our way out of it.

"Cost" is not a happy word. We usually equate it with loss. You must give up something you value to get what you want. "Pay" is no happier; it often equates with punishment. "You'll pay dearly for this." So when medical services have a "cost" and you "pay" for them, you are involved in a negative downward spiral.

I like the word "investment" a lot more. An investment implies that you are putting something in that will yield a greater return. When you plant a seed, you don't think of the seed as a cost or payment. You know that the seed is the beginning of something bigger and better than itself. It will grow to a phenomenally larger proportion. An apple seed is an investment in a huge apple tree that will bear fruit uncountably greater than its origin.

Your strongest investment in better health is your consciousness. When you love yourself enough to take care of yourself; know you deserve to feel good; hold the vision of a brilliantly functioning mind and body; quit engaging in activities that stress you and deplete your life force, and instead pursue activities that uplift and empower you; then you are planting seeds that will sprout and bear fruit many times greater. Paying a medical practitioner is the least investment in restoring, creating, or maintaining health. Visioning, praying, and right thinking, speaking, living, and loving will buy you far more health than money can purchase. At this moment the thoughts you are planting will grow into tomorrow's experience. Positive thinking is the most potent form of body building; every image you hold builds new cells and organs. Quit paying for good health and start investing in it.

God does not charge for healing. People do. Willingly pay doctors and healers for their services. They relieve pain, save and extend lives, and deserve our support. Meanwhile remember that it is your relationship with Higher Power that determines your well-being. Choose a doctor you believe in, has a good heart, and is more interested in helping than making money. One of my friends is a physician in India. When I asked her what she has learned about healing in her years of practice, she replied, "Love is the great healer." Love doesn't cost. Love only delivers blessings to the giver and receiver. God doesn't care about money. God cares about love. Money can't buy you health, but love can buy you happiness.

MASTER KEYS *of* THIS CHAPTER

1. Healing does not have to cost a lot of money or struggle. It can be free, inexpensive, and easy.

2. Many great healers, including spiritual healers and medical doctors, have given their services at little or no charge, and helped many people.

3. When you live in your natural state, physically and spiritually, you minimize your need for healing and you may not need to see a doctor or healer.

4. If you need to see a doctor, thank and bless that person for their services, and gratefully pay their fee, so they may be supported for their good work.

5. Hold your erroneous, fear-based ideas about money and healing up to the light of higher consciousness, that you may dissolve them and get clear about well-being and finances.

6. Healing does not require sacrifice. What heals you does not contain elements that hurt you. You can be healed naturally, without drugs or regimens with detrimental side effects.

7. Beware of healers who create false needs in patients in order to satisfy their profit motive.

8. Choose a healer who has a good heart and is dedicated to helping patients above all else. If you are a healer, keep service and kindness as your highest priorities.

WHY SOME PEOPLE
DON'T GET HEALED

Change is never painful.
Only resistance to change is painful.

—ATTRIBUTED TO BUDDHA

If healing is our natural state, everyone deserves it, and wellness is the will of God, why do some people not get healed? Why do some very kind and loving people struggle to survive, while many greedy and selfish people prosper? Why would a brilliant mind like Dr. Stephen Hawking be confined to a contorted body, and humanitarian Princess Diana die at a young age, while the pilot who dropped the atomic bomb on Hiroshima lived to a healthy 92, and swore that he never lost a night's sleep in the aftermath of what many people consider to be the most heinous single act of violence in human history?

I won't attempt to cite a simple glib answer to such pressing questions; their explanations are too complex to be unraveled in one swoop. But I can shed light on the components of consciousness that yield healing and the factors that work against it.

To begin, let's recognize that health or its absence do not occur at random. Wellness and illness represent choices by which the mind uses the body to play out beliefs and intentions. Edgar Cayce said, "Mind is the builder." We might extrapolate, "Mind is the sickener" and "Mind is the healer." Just as fingers animate a glove that has no will of its own, thoughts animate the body that is neutral.

Why, then, would a mind choose illness over wellness? Surely anyone in his right mind would prefer to be healthy. But few of us live in our right mind all the time. Everyone harbors at least a small cache of illusions that cause us to act in self-defeating ways or hurt others. More bluntly stated, most of us live in a mire of illusions most of the time. The world is a collage of photoshopped fantasies that warp reality into bizarre unnatural forms and twist happy dreams into nightmares. To be liberated from illness, we must courageously march into the basement of our subconscious, discover what is driving our pain, and transform limiting beliefs.

Here are seven ways we deny or delay healing, and how to offset them:

1. You regard sickness as a punishment for sin. If you believe in an angry, wrathful God, you will see yourself as guilty, and interpret pain as a penalty for your transgressions. When my mother was recovering from a surgery, she was in a lot of pain. She said, "I must have done something really bad to deserve this." My heart broke to hear this. My mom was a wonderful, loving woman who tried her best to be kind to everyone. The idea of her being punished by a vengeful God was inconceivable to me. But she was a Jewish mother well versed in the martial art of guilt, so she filtered her experience through the lens of retribution. At some point each of us must decide if God is cruel or loving; if creation is benign or dangerous. Einstein stated that the most fundamental question a person could ask is, "Is the universe a friendly place?" If you have children, you take no delight in their pain; to the contrary, your sole wish is for them to be happy and thrive. If we, in our shortsighted humanness, are capable of such a core intention for our children's wellness, would the Creator of the universe take a perverse pleasure in our suffering?

It is not God who punishes us, but we who punish ourselves. We believe that our pain pays off our guilt. *A Course in Miracles* tells us that if you never felt guilty, you would not know illness. Innocent people do not deserve to suffer. Yet, feeling guilty, we believe that if we mete out self-punishment, we can avoid God's harsher punishment, so we attempt to beat God at the game. We irrationally believe that illness buys us freedom.

To find healing, we must rise above a punishment mentality. We must cease to see ourselves as sinful and deserving of pain or lack of any kind. Yes, we make errors, but errors do not require punishment. They simply call for correction. When we correct our errors, we master the lessons the situation came to impart, and we are free. God does not punish. God heals. God is not the source of our pain. God is the answer to it.

2. You believe that sickness pays off your bad karma. The idea of karmic retribution is a slightly sanitized version of sin and punishment. It rises beyond the idea of God as a volatile father, and depicts our well-being or its lack as more scientific than emotional. Karma is easier to work with than sin and punishment, as it regards us less as a victim of external forces, and more at the helm of our destiny. We are not subservient to a violent, vengeful parent, but more at cause of the effects we generate. Sins send us to hell forever; karma gives us a chance to balance our account. Western Judeo-Christian versions of sin give us one life to get it right or be cast into the fiery pit forever. Eastern karma, embracing reincarnation, allows us to return until we get it right.

Yet the idea of karma is often twisted to cloak sin and punishment. I hear people far more often say, "This must be my bad karma coming back to haunt me" rather than "Wow! I must have some good karma for this to happen." We may also take a smug satisfaction in thinking vengefully about someone who has wronged us, "His karma will come back to get him."

When we reframe karma as a helpful balancing process, the system becomes our friend. When we are aligned with the Tao, the great stream of well-being, the universe works in our favor, we are healthy, and life is good. When we step away from the Tao and try to fight our way upstream, we get battered. Not as a punishment, but as a message from the universe saying, "The direction you are taking is not working. Try another way." If we are open and willing to try the other way, we get back into the positive stream.

It is tempting to use the idea of karma as an excuse to remain stuck. *"I guess it's just my karma to [stay sick] [work at this depressing job] [be in an abusive relationship]."* But if you are willing to assume responsibility for your life, you can rise above old bad karma and make new good karma. While karma may have contributed to you getting sick, grace will contribute to you getting well. Grace means you have access to a reality far greater than karma. Love can heal in a moment what karma created over years or lifetimes. Only you can keep yourself stuck; no one is doing it to you. When you are ready to break free, you will receive miraculous help from a Higher Hand.

Whether your karma is "good" or "bad" is a matter of interpretation, not fact. What initially appears to be bad can turn out to be very good. No situation has any implicit meaning. All the meaning we see is what we project. You can apply negative or positive meaning to any situation, and you will find more of the same.

My Japanese client Hiro told me, "Ever since I was a young man, I wanted to have children. When my first wife was infertile, I divorced her. I remarried and had a child with my second wife, but the child is disabled. I believe that my daughter's disability is a curse on me for divorcing my first wife."

"Do you love your daughter?" I asked Hiro.

"More than I can say. She is the light of my life."

"How has your relationship with her helped you grow?"

"I have more compassion. I have to slow down to help her with her daily activities. I am learning patience and focus. I see her beauty even beyond her disability."

"It sounds like your daughter is an angel come to bless you rather than a devil come to curse you."

"Yes, I can see that now."

Do not be hasty to judge challenging situations as bad karma. Your karma is what you make it by means of the thoughts you think about it. Most people consider karma to be horizontal, a chain of sequential events in time; you act now, and results return sooner or later. While this is so, the deeper dynamic of karma is vertical. A situation comes before you, you think about it in a certain way, and you instantly reap the results of the way you are thinking about it. In this sense, all karma is instant in that you experience the effects of your thoughts the moment you think them. Thus you can change your karma at any given moment by changing the way you are thinking about a person or event.

3. The perceived rewards of illness exceed the rewards of wellness. Every human being is doing what he believes yields the greatest benefit. But if the person's motivation is dysfunctional, he may choose behaviors or habits that ultimately cause greater pain to himself or others. Sugar, heroin, and gambling deliver a quick rush of pleasure, but then cost the person far more in the long run. People in abusive relationships find a certain safety or security they fear they would lose if they left. Women who sacrifice their lives for their husband or family, or religious fanatics who mutilate their flesh, believe that their loss buys a greater gain. Despite appearances, we live entirely by choice, often self-destructively.

In my book *A Course in Miracles Made Easy,* I explain the perceived payoffs of sickness in great detail. For now, I will list them briefly:

- You don't have to go to work, school, or engage in activities you detest.
- You get attention.
- You get sympathy.
- You get favors, like ice cream when as a child you stayed home from school, sick.
- You get money.
- You prove that a person, event, or institution has done you wrong.
- You prove that you are a victim of your body, and you avoid responsibility for the decisions of your mind.
- You get social respect and honor for being hurt for a good cause. "The red badge of courage." You get a license plate honoring you for being wounded.

The fact that people choose illness does not mean we should not help sick people, have compassion, deny financial support for disabilities, or provide special access. Nor does it mean we should overlook our own pain, push on to override symptoms, or beat ourselves up for getting sick. Kindness to self and others is a huge spiritual lesson we all do well to practice. The responsibility for health means that we need to look deeper into why we might be at choice about illness rather than perceive ourselves as its victim. The word "attack" is terribly misapplied when it comes to illness, such as "heart attack" or "asthma attack." The heart does not attack us. We attack ourselves. The heart is an innocent vital organ simply trying to do its job. Its pain is a plea for attention, care, and perhaps a change in lifestyle. It does not want to hurt you. It wants you to quit hurting yourself. The body is not our enemy. It is our friend. When we treat it with respect, it will treat us respectfully and function well.

4. You find wellness scarier than illness. If you have developed an identity or lifestyle around limited health, you might find it threatening to be cast into freedom. The ego's motto is "The known is always preferable to the unknown, even if the known sucks." In the film *The Legend of 1900,* a baby born on a cruise ship is abandoned and raised by the ship's crew. The boy finds a welcome home on the ship and grows up to be an accomplished musical performer. For his entire youth he never steps off the ship onto shore. Then he falls in love with a passenger and deeply yearns to follow her home. But when the time comes, he cannot bring himself to walk the gangplank to land. Even though he is confined to an extremely limited environment, he equates it with safety, and the world outside, though it offers far vaster potential, seems dangerous.

While the story is a parable, the dynamic is quite practical. If you have built a lifestyle around a limitation, freedom from your familiar world may seem threatening and you might choose the illness lifestyle instead.

5. You give your power to negative diagnoses and prognoses. When a doctor diagnoses an illness, advises you what you need to do to heal it, predicts the time it will take to heal, or cites its incurability, his advice proceeds from three factors: (1) his beliefs; (2) his experience; and (3) statistics he has read about how that disease has affected others. While all of this information is accurate within his belief system and he is being honest about what he knows, there are many more factors that affect your healing process. I have stated that there exist many parallel realities, each self-affirming for those who subscribe to it. If you dwell in the same reality the doctor is citing, his prognosis will likely be correct. Yet there is one factor that statistics never take into account: the consciousness and intention of the patient. If you eat the same empty diet, watch the same morbid newscasts, stream the same violent movies, become embroiled in the same political arguments, place yourself in the same toxic environments, dwell on the same fearful thoughts, and maintain the same lifestyle as the masses upon which the statistics are based, you will probably have the same experience. If, however, you choose more uplifting thoughts, recognize the presence of the healing power that animates the entire universe, avoid depressing news and conversations, select uplifting entertainment, treat your body lovingly, choose healthy environments, and have a strong intention to heal, you are not subject to the cited statistics or prognosis. Statistics apply to the masses, not individuals. If you are reading this book, you are likely an independent thinker and you recognize possibilities that span far beyond the norm.

A disease may linger because you believe it will take a long time to heal. In some cases, your belief may be accurate, since you may have run down an organ and it will take some time to regenerate. Don't be disappointed or beat yourself up if you do not experience healing overnight. It is also possible to have an instantaneous healing. I know many people who have had cancer and other diseases disappear in a flash, leaving doctors scratching their heads, citing "spontaneous remission," which means, "medicine has no explanation for something that happened by a mysterious higher power." I know of a woman who was deeply addicted to heroin, her life in such a tailspin that she turned to prostitution to support her habit. In desperation, she went to a class on energy healing and she was able to entirely free herself from the habit very quickly, with no withdrawal symptoms, a progression that is medically impossible.

You can minimize your susceptibility to disease by refusing to become immersed in mass thoughts about it. My teacher Hilda never read the newspaper on the same day it was printed. "When the news comes out, everyone who reads it is concentrating on the same bad news and adding their emotion to it," she explained. "A day or two later, people have gotten over the story and they are on to the next one. I prefer not to read news polluted by humanity's upset. There are better things to think and feel about."

Hilda's idea was corroborated by an experiment in which psychologists took a group of crossword puzzle aficionados and tested their ability to solve the *New York Times* crossword puzzle of the day. Several days later the same group was asked to solve the *Times* puzzle of the previous day (which they had not yet seen). The puzzle solvers did significantly better on the day-old puzzle than they had done on the same-day puzzle. After the puzzle had been solved by many people, the answers were established in the group mind, or race thought. The puzzle doers were able to tap into the results imbedded by those who had solved the puzzle on the day it was released. The day-after subjects took advantage of the group mind.

For every disease humanity knows, some people have been healed of that ailment, demonstrating that no disease is absolutely incurable. Never accept a doctor's prediction that you must stay sick for any length of time, or die. If you choose exceptional thoughts, you will reap exceptional results. Neither give your power away to the negative fore-cast of a psychic, fortune teller, or astrologer. You, not your stars, numbers, or personality type are in charge of your destiny. *Your* mind and *your* choices create *your* destiny, which external situations play out. Change your mind, and seemingly external causes become external effects.

6. You continue to engage in the behavior that caused the illness. Illness is stress related. A part of the body is over-worked, overwhelmed, or undernourished because fear, resistance, or maltreatment has diminished your natural flow of life force. If you continue to stress that part of the body, it cannot heal. Give the body a chance to restore itself by letting that organ rest and renew. The Power within you will do its miraculous job. Examine, too, the patterns of thought and emotion that fuel your stress. When you allevi-ate stress at the core level, the body will re-form itself often quickly, without struggle or strain.

7. You have a soul contract. Before you were born, you decided you would learn certain important lessons during your journey through the material world. Some of those les-sons are founded in joy, and others show up as challenges. Having an illness or physical disability may be one way you achieve profound learning, such as self-honoring, accepting love and support, perseverance, compassion, setting healthy boundaries, expressing your true choices, or recognizing your identity as a spiritual being not limited by your physi-cal experience. You might also learn that you didn't need to be sick at all; you could have accomplished the same learn-ing in a healthy body.

Yet take care not to use the idea of a soul contract to perpetuate illness. Don't write off your illness as required because your soul chose it. You can potentially change a soul contract. A key element of your contract may have been to learn how to transcend it and renegotiate a new contract based on well-being. (For a thorough exploration of how soul contracts work, see my book *Soul and Destiny.*)

We make decisions at a deep level we cannot understand at the shallower level of the thinking mind. The intellect, wondrous, resourceful, and practical as it is, is an extremely limited tool for understanding the universe. The intellect helps us survive and navigate the physical world, but it does not penetrate to the causational level of life. There are far deeper and more rewarding ways to understand and master the universe. As Antoine de Saint-Exupéry nobly stated in his classic novella *The Little Prince,* "It is only with the heart that one can see rightly; what is essential is invisible to the eye."

Quit Finding Reasons for Illness

While it can be helpful to understand why illness occurs and why we perpetuate it, eventually we must grow beyond seeking reasons for disease and we must seek and find reasons for wellness. We will not achieve healing by immersing ourselves in the study of illness. Scientists have been studying illness for thousands of years, and have had success in offsetting many diseases. Still much of humanity remains ill and the number of new and different diseases continues to increase. This is because we maintain limiting beliefs related to disease and, on some level, we keep choosing it. Disease can be represented by iron filings clinging to an electromagnet. As long as the magnet is energized, the filings remain stuck to it. When the electromagnet is turned off, the filings drop away. Our mind is the magnet and symptoms are the filings. By another analogy, two pieces of Velcro stick together because their hooks are configured to interlock. If one piece of Velcro becomes worn or flaccid, the hooks no longer interlock and the pieces fall away from each other. A mindset of illness or belief in its value is represented by one side of the Velcro, and the symptoms of illness are represented by the other side. Change your mental configuration, and the disease has nothing to hook to. Disease and wellness function at two entirely different frequencies. Raise your frequency above disease and it will have no home in your world.

Some doctors will not stop examining you until they find something wrong with you. They have been trained to look for diseases, not health. While this procedure makes sense if you are in pain and you need to find what is causing it, searching for problems can be overindulged. I received a letter of thanks from the director of an internationally-respected holistic medical clinic. He liked an idea I published: "Choose a doctor who will find something right with you."

Mass Subconscious Choices for Disease

While individuals may find dysfunctional value in holding onto a disease, we also perpetuate disease by mass agreement. Many people benefit from the diseases of others, primarily by receiving payments for their treatment. Patients' diseases keep doctors, pharmaceutical companies, hospitals, and related industries in business. If people got healed, such professionals would be out of jobs.

Imagine you work as a physician, nurse, technician, administrator, or in any service related to a particular disease that many people have. Your livelihood depends on people continuing to have that disease. Then imagine one day you open your web browser or newspaper and the headline reads, "Science has found a definitive cure for [the disease you treat]." While on one level you might be happy for all the people who would now be relieved of that burden, on a subconscious level you might freak out. All the income you gain for your family, home, and life just disappeared. You may have to sell your home and find an entirely different way to earn a living. While most people working in the medical profession are kind, caring professionals who sincerely want their patients to get healed, there simultaneously exists a mass subconscious survival mechanism that perceives reward from that disease, and regards the disease disappearing as a threat.

Dr. Michael Klaper, the vegan nutrition expert I mentioned earlier, relates that at a large Midwest hospital, 14 of the hospital's 25 cardiologists have adopted a vegan diet - and they encourage their heart patients to do the same. As a result, many patients are getting healed and not returning to the hospital. When this trend became apparent, the hospital's chief cardiologist was called in by the administration and told that his physicians would have to find a way to keep their patients coming back or else the unit would have to cut back on its staff and services. The tail is wagging the dog.

Doctors should be rewarded for curing their patients' diseases, not perpetuating them. I heard about a Chinese medical system in which people pay doctors as long as they stay healthy. When a person becomes ill, she no longer pays the doctor, giving him an incentive to help her get well again. While this system offers an attractive alternative to our current system, it is not without flaw. In this case, patients rather than doctors are rewarded for keeping their illness. As long as anyone is rewarded for illness, a system is susceptible to abuse. In an ideal world, doctors would treat patients at no charge and be sustained by the community for their services.

The Deepest Level of Healing

Dr. Jerry Jampolsky is a psychiatrist whose life was profoundly changed by his study of *A Course in Miracles*. As a result, he transformed his practice to serve families of children with catastrophic illnesses. Dr. Jampolsky established the Center for Attitudinal Healing, which now has outlets in many countries. He defines healing as inner peace. If your body is functioning properly but you do not have inner peace, you cannot say you are healed. If your body is not working but you have inner peace, healing has occurred. Real healing is of the mind more than the body.

When I worked in a veteran's hospital, I met a patient named Willie, who spent his days in a wheelchair as a quadriplegic. While Willie's physical capacities were quite limited, he had an extraordinarily positive attitude and always had a kind word for the other patients and the hospital staff, who were overworked and grouchy. Physically, Willie was disabled. Mentally, emotionally, and spiritually, he was magnificently vital and joyful. Willie provided living proof that health and happiness are more a function of the mind than the body. I later heard about a paraplegic man who founded an organization called, "Disabled—but Not Really." Even while disability appears physically real, spiritually we are all entirely abled.

There is far more to who gets healed and who does not, than meets the eye. There is an element of choice behind illness that few people recognize. While some would argue that illness is not a choice, accepting this choice is the key to escape from pain. If you are powerful enough to make yourself sick, you are powerful enough to make yourself well. If you have the capacity to cut yourself off from the source of wellness, you also have the capacity to reunite with it. The great illusion is that the world happens to you. The great truth is that you happen to the world, including your body in the world. God loved you enough to give you the power to choose healing. You return that gift by choosing it.

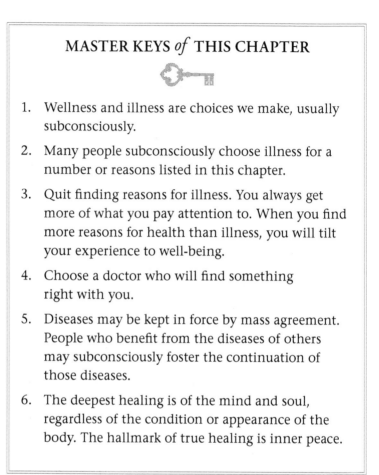

MASTER KEYS *of* THIS CHAPTER

1. Wellness and illness are choices we make, usually subconsciously.

2. Many people subconsciously choose illness for a number or reasons listed in this chapter.

3. Quit finding reasons for illness. You always get more of what you pay attention to. When you find more reasons for health than illness, you will tilt your experience to well-being.

4. Choose a doctor who will find something right with you.

5. Diseases may be kept in force by mass agreement. People who benefit from the diseases of others may subconsciously foster the continuation of those diseases.

6. The deepest healing is of the mind and soul, regardless of the condition or appearance of the body. The hallmark of true healing is inner peace.

DEFEATING THE ARMIES OF FEAR

The enemy is fear. We think it is hate; but, it is fear.

—MAHATMA GANDHI

Bruno Gröning caused a huge stir in Germany in 1949 when he healed a boy of severe muscular dystrophy. When word quickly spread about Gröning's extraordinary abilities, thousands of people flocked to him, beseeching him for healing. At one point 30,000 people gathered outside his house, waiting day and night for him to appear, deliver soothing words, and relieve their misery. To a large extent, he did. The lame walked, the blind saw, the deaf heard, and all manner of ailments deemed incurable were banished. Gröning was a true purveyor of miracles.

Tragically, the German medical establishment was extremely threatened by this gentle Christ-like figure. Although Gröning never accepted any money, did not touch people, did not prescribe medicine, gave God all credit for the healings, and did not speak against doctors—he encouraged people to see them—the authorities accused him of practicing medicine without a license. They banned the man from performing healing, and waged numerous lawsuits against him. Gröning responded with dignity and refrained from healing, despite the fact that many highly respected doctors and medical authorities testified in his favor and the public cried out for him to carry on. Gröning stated that if he was not allowed to pass along healing energy to people who needed it, he would "burn up inside." Alas, by 1959 he developed stomach cancer and passed away at the age of 53. A doctor who performed a surgery on Gröning announced that he had never seen an organ appear so charred.

The insane ban on Gröning's healing is not surprising. Jesus Christ offered boundless healing to the people of his time, but the Romans and the Jewish religious leaders considered him a threat, so he was crucified. Bruno Gröning was also crucified, not on a cross, but slowly through modern legal proceedings. The execution device was different, the result the same.

Many others who attempted to advance society's well-being have been mowed down by fear. Abraham Lincoln, Gandhi, Martin Luther King Jr., the Kennedys, and countless saints and healers have met with violent resistance and death. Yet their legacy lives on. You can kill a body, but not an idea. You can do away with a person, but not a spirit. You can legislate against healing, but not stop it. Because healing is our natural state, eventually it must prevail.

The Extinction Burst

When you take a step toward healing, everything unlike healing tends to show up to oppose it. In behavioral psychology, this process is called an *extinction burst*. If you give a dog a treat every time it whines for one, and then you withhold the treat, the dog's whining will increase dramatically. If you refrain from giving in, eventually the dog will realize that more whining will not get it what it wants, and it will give up the annoying habit. Homeopathic doctors call this process the Herxheimer Reaction. Bruno Gröning dubbed it *Regelungen*, or "regulation." He explained that symptoms may exacerbate before they are purged. My teacher used to say, "The plant is most bitter at the root." The darkest hour is just before the dawn.

Do not be put off by resistance to healing, within you or around you. The bolder the step forward, the greater the opposition to it. British novelist Jonathan Swift stated, "When a true genius appears, you can know him by this sign: that all the dunces are in a confederacy against him." Einstein echoed, "Great spirits have always encountered violent opposition from mediocre minds." The Wright brothers' father was a fundamentalist preacher who warned his sons that their experiments to develop a flying machine were the work of the devil. "If God wanted us to fly, he would have given us wings." Maybe. But He also might have given us airplanes. Few people remember the Wright brothers' father, but billions of people appreciate being able to fly.

Ironically, some of the most stalwart opponents of healing are often those who claim to deliver it. When a natural healer shows up, doctors and priests are the first to deny the positive results. In Bruno Gröning's case, the medical establishment was his biggest enemy. Likewise, the church is often the foremost denier of miracles. Consider the miraculous apparitions that occurred in Garabandal, Portugal, from 1961 to 1965. Similar to the apparitions at Fatima, four young girls experienced repeated visions of the Virgin Mary. In the middle of the night they were each awakened from their respective homes at the same time, and walked trance-like to a glen near their humble village, where Mother Mary revealed herself and gave them teachings, advice, and prophecies. When word got around, hordes of people followed them to observe the miraculous events. Many people experienced healings of body and soul, and countless lives were changed for the better. You would think that the Church would have been thrilled to celebrate such wonderful encounters. But no. If you report a miracle to the Catholic Church, there is a long, convoluted, almost unsurpassable process you have to go through to get the event acknowledged as a miracle. Even while thousands of people have experienced healings and found renewed faith in God through the Garabandal apparitions, the Church has refused to acknowledge divine presence in those encounters. Fortunately, God does not need any church's approval to achieve the many miracles and healings that go on every day.

Charlie Goldsmith is a humble Australian man in whose presence many people have been healed. An investigative television show tested Goldsmith's healing ability by bringing a group of ill people to him. Goldsmith was successful in healing most of them, in particular an eleven-year-old girl who had suffered with juvenile arthritis since she was sixteen months of age. The girl stated that she had pain everywhere in her body. After a few minutes in Goldsmith's presence, her symptoms disappeared. Meanwhile a skeptical doctor looked on sternly. He concluded that because the methodology could not be proven, the treatment and results were not valid. Meanwhile tears of joy streamed down the girl's face, her mother's, and that of the audience. In contrast to the skeptical doctor, another physician with 30 years' experience stated, "I can't explain it. I saw it, so therefore I must believe it." The show conducted a follow-up a length of time after Charlie's treatment, and the girl, along with others who had been subject to long-time chronic pain, reported that their symptoms had not recurred. The girl was now running, dancing, and jumping, pain free. (YouTube: "Healer or Hoax? Charlie Goldsmith Put to the Test") What science could not explain, Spirit manifested. Lesson 76 of *A*

Course in Miracles urges us to recognize, "I am under no laws but God's."

You don't need a doctor or church to approve your healing. If God approves your healing, you are good to go. God doesn't belong to any particular medical practice or religion. God belongs to all doctors and all religions. Open-minded physicians and clergy will celebrate your healing with you, and the closed-minded will deny it. So what? You don't need anyone's permission to be well. You just need God's and your own. You already have God's. The rest is up to you.

How to Move Beyond Resistance

Whenever you step forward to claim a big new "yes," your old "no's" come back to greet you. Thus resistance is a sign that you are on the verge of a breakthrough. The old limited self realizes that it is about to be replaced by a broader, freer self, so it marshals every trick it knows to keep you enclosed within the circle of fear you dare not move beyond. But when you find the courage to step over the line, you realize that it was drawn by illusion, not truth. Fear is the liar. Wellness is the truth about who you are and what you deserve. Einstein further stated, "The mediocre mind is incapable of understanding the man who refuses to bow blindly to conventional prejudices and chooses instead to express his opinions courageously and honestly." Likewise, the mediocre part of our mind is incapable to understand and support the part of us that chooses to step forth to express wellness, love, and prosperity. Define those three attributes as the truth about you, and all else as the anomaly, and you will move boldly and rapidly to fulfill your destiny.

Here are some signs of resistance to healing or life changes calling you to step forward:

1. Exaggerated physical symptoms of the illness you are seeking to heal

2. New symptoms of other maladies

3. Irritability and argumentativeness

4. Depression

5. Fatigue

6. Threats or adversity by people who play out your fears and judgments

7. A tendency to fall back on addictive behaviors like overeating, drinking, drugging, overworking, obsessive sex, or screen time

8. The belief that there is something you need to finish, achieve, or fix before you can heal

9. Emergencies or dramas that threaten to stop you from moving ahead

I observe the latter phenomenon with students who sign up for my Life Coach Training Program or another intensive residential retreat. It is quite common for our office to receive an email or phone call from a student who has some drama unexpectedly arise a day or two before she is about to step on the airplane to come to the program. Someone in the family is sick; a colleague at work quits or a project falls through; an unexpected bill comes in; ex-husband doesn't want to assume child care; and all kinds of variations on these themes. While sometimes these emergencies are valid reasons for a participant to not show up, most of the time such situations are manifestations of fear and resistance. In such cases I or one of my staff explains the extinction burst dynamic to the participant and we encourage her to move ahead anyway. Most of the time she does, and she is glad she did. The drama gets handled and the participant has a transformational experience at the program. In retrospect, the student realizes that a part of her recognized that her life was about to change for the better, and the part of her mind that feared change was making a desperate last stand.

Here are some tips on how to move through such resistance:

1. Notice and acknowledge it.

2. Do your best to view the resistance dispassionately without getting caught up in it.

3. Express your experience to someone you trust and whose support you value.

4. Take whatever reasonable measures you can to address the symptoms or the issue.

5. Pray, meditate, and ask for guidance from Higher Power.

6. Engage in self-nurturing activities that raise your frequency and put you in a more relaxed state.

7. Be patient with yourself and anyone else involved.

8. Do an introspective analysis: "What fear is manifesting through this symptom? What is the lie that is fueling the fear? What is the truth the lie is covering? What would love, self-confidence, and trust guide me to do?"

9. Move ahead anyway.

My mentor painted a metaphorical picture: "The dogs bark, and the caravan moves on." Your move ahead is the caravan, and your fears or reasons to stay stuck are the barking dogs. A step in a positive direction is far more powerful than any resistance to it. Instead of fantasizing about all the things that could go wrong, fantasize about all the things that could go right. How great could your life get if you moved forward? Because health is stronger than illness and peace is closer to your true nature than pain, when you connect with your spiritual Source, you become unstoppable.

Rise Above

If you battle resistance, the resistance has won. Jesus advised, "Resist not evil, but overcome evil with good." Resistance is not defeated by more resistance; it is surpassed by rising above it. This dynamic applies not just to resistance coming from outside you, but also to resistance arising from within you. Fighting negativity keeps you tied to it. "Never wrestle with a pig. You both get dirty, and the pig likes it." Rather than regarding resistance as a powerful enemy, treat it like a petulant child. At Disneyland, parents are given hand leashes to keep their little children from wandering off and getting lost or hurt. Keep your resistance on a short leash, or else it will drag you to painful, nonproductive, and dangerous places. Give it a little space to express itself, but do not allow it to rule your magic kingdom. When your commitment to healing is stronger than the part of your mind committed to keeping you from it, wellness and success will become your prevalent experiences.

The Legacy of Great Healers

Although Jesus' body disappeared two millennia ago, his healing power goes on, and many people are healed in his name daily. While Bruno Gröning passed away over a half-century ago, to this day many people who tap into

Gröning's energy have been miraculously hea
umentation to support their cures. (www.bri
org/en/healings/physical healings) So it is wil
healers who have departed, or living healers who neai at a
distance. It is not the body or personality that accomplishes
the healing. It is the healer's connection to universal life
force, which is everywhere. A true healer is not defined by his
physical form or limited to it. The death of Jesus, Gröning,
or any healer is inconsequential compared to their presence
and power to heal. Like a star that continues to radiate light
far into the universe for eons after it has gone nova, true
healers continue to bless the world long after their bodies
disappear.

The crucifixion of Christ or Gröning was a lesser scene
in a greater play. As givers of life, those master souls want
us to focus on the vitality they brought to the world rather
than their demise. The radiant, smiling, open-armed Christ
is a far more fitting model of his teaching than his limp,
bloodied form nailed to a cross. Any form of fear or crucifixion you experience is small change in contrast to your power
and mission to heal. God cannot be crucified. Only the ego
resists God, rattling its tin foil sabers in its petty kingdom
that God dismisses with a sigh and a laugh. God lives far
beyond any challenge. God simply is, and the pure positive
energy that God is, heals. All other stories are footnotes to
the Bible of Grace.

MASTER KEYS *of* THIS CHAPTER

1. Some people, motivated by fear, do not wish to see others healed. They may actively fight or try to do away with genuine healers and healing technologies.

2. The closer an individual or society comes to healing, the more darkness magnifies and tries to thwart the light. The greater the resistance to wellness, the closer to healing.

3. Sometimes the institutions that are intended to foster wellness, such as the church or the medical establishment, most actively deny or resist demonstrations of healing.

4. Events that seem to thwart healing are often signs that you are on the verge of a breakthrough.

5. When you experience resistance to healing, you can move ahead in a number of effective ways listed in this chapter.

6. Although many great healers have been thwarted or assassinated, their healing legacy goes on, gathering force and healing long after the healer has departed.

TOO BLESSED TO
BE STRESSED

When you realize how perfect everything is,
you will tilt your head back and laugh at the sky.

—ATTRIBUTED TO BUDDHA

The stirring film *Apollo 11* documents many little-known details of humanity's first journey to walk on the moon. One fascinating fact revealed was the pulse rate of the crew upon takeoff. As the behemoth Saturn 5 rocket blasted off from the Kennedy Space Center launch pad with 7.5 million pounds of thrust, mission control remotely monitored the heartbeats of the astronauts in the tiny capsule intensely vibrating atop the 320-foot-tall rocket. As expected, the heartbeats of astronauts Neil Armstrong and Michael Collins were quite high—over 110 beats per minute—to be expected at such a trying moment. Meanwhile, astronaut Buzz Aldrin's pulse registered at just 82 beats per minute—not much higher than in a fully relaxed situation. I find it fascinating that a man could be in circumstances that would severely rattle most human beings, and still be nearly perfectly relaxed—a powerful demonstration that stress and relaxation are the result more of choices than circumstances.

While you and I do not sit atop a monster shaking rocket, we have many opportunities each day to choose peace over upset. *A Course in Miracles* asks us to affirm, "I could see peace instead of this." Blessing and stressing cannot dwell at any given moment in the same soul. The two experiences represent alternate realities with no overlap. Blessing is liberating and healing, and stress is confining and debilitating. You can't have a little bit of hell in heaven. The Course further reminds us, "Only the creations of light are real. Everything else is your own nightmare."

Spiritual Immunity

The U.S. Navy conducted an experiment with astounding, far-reaching implications. Seeking to discover a cure for influenza, the Navy solicited 50 young sailors to volunteer to contract the disease and be monitored as to the disease's progression. The sailors were sent to Goat Island, where they were injected with influenza bacteria, inhaled influenza-laden air, and interacted intensively with influenza patients. The doctors who conducted the experiment watched and waited for the sailors to exhibit symptoms of the disease so they could be studied.

Then something amazing happened: Not one of the 50 sailors contracted influenza. They all remained perfectly healthy. While doctors scratched their heads as to why the sailors did not get sick, there is a metaphysical explanation: they had no fear or resistance to the disease. They were confident they would be okay even if they got sick. Fear lowers resistance and plummets us to a consciousness of vulnerability, which increases our chances of being affected by the thing we fear. Deep trust, faith, and confidence that we are whole, well, and protected increases our immunity to the point that we become invulnerable.

I related this fascinating story to a Japanese doctor who directs an influenza clinic. He told me that he has run this clinic for ten years, interacting intensively with flu patients. Not once during that time has he contracted the flu.

When you live in the consciousness of innate well-being, dwelling in the presence of God wherever you go, you retain your natural state of wholeness, and adverse conditions cannot reach, touch, or hurt you.

I am not suggesting that you put yourself in situations you believe might harm you or engage in health practices you believe unsafe. It is the very belief in harm that attracts harm. I am suggesting that you drop into the deep knowingness that your true self is eternally whole, untouchable by any external agent, and no matter what is going on in the world around you, you remain as God created you.

Start Destressing Now

One significant step you can take toward healing, easily within your command, is to conduct an honest introspection of where stress exists in your life, and then take whatever steps you can to alleviate it. As you lighten up even a little, you will notice a difference in your attitude, energy, and health. You may not experience a miraculous healing instantly (or you might), but you will begin to reverse the debilitating effects of stress. Unless you have a medical emergency, you may do well to do what you can to destress before you go to a doctor or take a drug. If you have an emergency, or you destress and you still need help, by all means get professional support. You will be gratified, even amazed, to see how your well-being improves when you relax.

The word "disease" contains a hidden clue to healing. Break the word down to "dis-ease" and you will understand its message: Ease is our natural state, how we were born to live. When we drop into fear, upset, guilt, pressure, or resistance, we diss ease. When we reclaim ease, we begin to restore our natural well-being. The dynamic is quite simple—unless you wish to complicate it.

While it may appear that stress is situational—you have too many tasks before you, too many obligations, too much pressure, and not enough time, money, energy, or resources to get it all done—it is more attitudinal. All of life is attitudinal. What appears to be the world is simply a projection of the beliefs we are using to view it. Some people are extremely busy and surf through a myriad of projects and responsibilities. They hold a lighthearted attitude, feel good, enjoy abundant energy, laugh a lot, and gracefully execute their work and family obligations. Others feel overwhelmed by just about any task that comes before them. Their work and family pose a drudgery, they are tired and sick, have little fun, and groan at the prospect of waking up to face another bleary day. It's not what we do that creates stress. It's *why* and *how* we do it.

While you may not be able to change the people and situations around you, or make certain obligations go away, you have the power to upgrade your attitude toward them. Sometimes you can change your environment. Always you can change your mind. Work from the level of mind, and the other levels will follow.

To begin destressing, ask yourself these key questions:

What do I really need to do, and what is optional?

Which tasks need to be done today, and which can wait?

Am I laying extra tasks or unrealistic deadlines
over what is actually required?

Which tasks proceed from "should,"
and which proceed from "would?"

Which of the tasks before me are joy-motivated,
and which are fear-motivated?

Is there some way I could approach my necessary
tasks with a lighter, more playful attitude?

If I were living truer to my values, joy, and authentic
choices, what would I be doing differently?

If I tore up my to-do list, how would I be spending my day?

As you answer these questions, you will probably realize that a certain amount of the stress you experience—maybe all of it—is self-imposed. It may appear that other people and the world are oppressing you with obligations, but you are more oppressing yourself. If others are making too many demands upon you, on some level you are agreeing with them and demanding of yourself. Even while there are tasks you must do, you may be burdening yourself with fear, guilt, resentment, or self-criticism for not being a perfect achiever. Perhaps ancient voices of demanding parents or other authority figures haunt you, psychically whipping you for not meeting the impossible standards they set. Yet when you step back and rationally evaluate your endless list of tasks, you realize that you will never get them all done. For every goal you complete in the world, more show up to replace it. On the day you die, you will have emails in your inbox. Get over the idea that you will complete all the tasks before you; do what you can with ease, flow, and joy, and allow God to help you with rest. You have far more support than you realize. Enjoy life right where you stand. Real success is not about completion of tasks. It is about elevation of attitude.

The Great Escape

Here are some ways to undo stress from the inside out, and find your way to blessing and healing:

(1) Understand why you engage in unnecessary stressful activities. Such activities are always fear-based. You may fear being judged by others; or being punished by a spouse, boss, or God for not doing what they want you to do; or failing to meet unreasonable standards and expectations you set for yourself. You may be endlessly trying to prove yourself. You may also regard quiet and space as threatening. Blaise Pascal stated, "All of man's troubles stem from his inability to sit quietly in a room alone." Many people become busyholics because they are afraid that if they stopped running, they would have to face their self-doubts, self-judgments, or guilt; in the absence of frenzied activity your inner demons would arise to haunt, attack, or devour you.

Yet while dragon-like thoughts might rear their heads, if you face your fears with calm clarity, you will discover that they are all liars. Beneath your fears you will discover your impeccable beauty, loveableness, brilliance, and innocence. It is but fear that urges you to generate an endless parade of errands, tasks, dramas, and emergencies to avoid being with yourself. Ironically, the thing you fear the most would be the thing that heals you. In sacred silence you would unearth the riches of your soul, your inherent worthiness, and your priceless true self. Your quietude would not be a curse, but liberation.

(2) Affirm enoughness. You are stressed because you have given your power away to thoughts of lack. I used to believe I never had enough time to do all of my tasks and meetings. Meanwhile I recognized material abundance. One day

it occurred to me that if the universe is abundant in material wealth, it is also abundant in time. Either the universe is abundant or it is not. This is a fundamental decision you must make. If the universe is abundant, abundance is *everywhere*, including time. You cannot make an exception to truth and say, "universal principles apply in this quadrant of the universe, but not in that one." There are no pockets of creation where God is absent. We can make up stories that God cannot help our checkbook, datebook, or day planner, but that does not mean they are true. It just means we can use the power of our mind to keep supply at a distance. Meanwhile well-being awaits like a precious gift left on your doorstep waiting for you to open the door and receive it.

Here is an affirmation worth practicing until it sinks in as reality:

> I always have enough time to do the things
> that Spirit would have me do.

If the universe gives you a task, it will give you the time to do it. Contrary to what some religions teach, God does not pressure, demand, threaten, punish, test, or put you in positions that compromise your well-being. You may exert those demands on yourself, but God has nothing to do with them. All of those harrowing experiences are human fabrications. God's deepest desire is for you to prosper in every aspect of your life, including time. If you do not have enough time to get things done, you have superimposed extraneous needs on your to-do list. Tell the impeccable truth about what really needs to get done, and what doesn't. If something really needs to get done, you will have enough time to do it.

(3) Sort out the required from the optional.

Here is another affirmation that will work wonders as you apply it:

I can always do one thing less than I think I can.

It's not the required tasks that drive you crazy. It's the ones you sprinkle on top of the required tasks, the straws that break the camel's back. Shave off the unnecessary tasks, and just do what is absolutely required. If you don't need to do it today, leave it for tomorrow, or next week, or never. Focus on what's before you. Doing the task at hand well will lead to doing the next task well. Peeling away self-imposed obligations or deadlines will liberate time and energy for you to take care of what really needs to be done, with time to spare.

(4) Don't fill in free time with more work. We have invented miraculous labor- and time-saving technology, but then what do we do with the free time we liberated? Work more! How many times a day do you really need to check your text or email? How many errands do you really need to run? How many new projects do you need to initiate? How many people do you need to help before you can relax? While these activities may be helpful or fun, we can become so addicted to them that they rob us of energy rather than enlivening us. The fearful mind will fill in space with anything and everything to distract us from being fully present. Mindless activity debilitates. Full presence heals. When you take your last breath, you will not count the number of your Facebook friends. You will count the number of minutes you were present with the people you love.

(5) Partner with Higher Power. You are not in this alone. You have help from unseen sources and forces. *A Course in*

Miracles tells us, "If you knew who walks beside you on the path that you have chosen, fear would be impossible." A sense of isolation and feeling unsupported is debilitating. Knowing that you are connected to a brilliantly helpful and creative universe undoes fear and its effects.

If you face a task that feels or looms stressful, say, "Okay universe, I don't know if or how I can get this done. Would you please lend me a hand? I now humbly open to assistance from Higher Power. I am willing to be guided and comforted, and for the universe to help me take care of the things I cannot do by myself."

What self-respecting God would not answer a prayer like this? If your child came to you with a burdensome problem, fearful and worried, and asked you for help, would you not do everything in your power to support your child? And if we, in our abysmal humanness, are capable of such compassion, how much more does the God who created the heavens and earth love us? How capable is that Power to support, sustain, soothe, and heal us, and accomplish for us what we cannot accomplish for ourselves?

(6) *Find a way to play and dance through your responsibilities.* If you have to do a task you would prefer not to do, don't wear down your battery by resisting it. Resistance makes work harder and longer. Instead, make a game out of it. Find some way to be lighthearted as you move through it. When you lighten up, the task will seem less onerous, time will pass more quickly, and you will flow onto your next more joyful activity.

Is Some Stress Helpful?

Some psychologists suggest that some forms of stress are helpful. There is good stress and bad stress, they say. Good stress would motivate you to finish a project by a deadline or excel in a competition. But there is a difference between stress and motivation. You can be motivated without being stressed. Stress implies fear-based pressure, such as botching your presentation or not finding a mate by a certain age. By contrast, the excitement that stimulates a person to strive for a valued goal is different than the pressure of fearing to not achieve it. When you are inspired by joy to take an action, your body secretes the pleasure-inducing hormones I described earlier. When you are under stress, you drop into a primal fight-or-flight survival mechanism, fired by adrenaline. If the psychologists who lobby for good stress mean that a jolt of adrenaline can save your life if you are being chased by a tiger, they are correct. But we often interpret situations to be survival-threatening when they are not. You will not die if you don't get your final exam in on time. The fearful mind goes to the worst-case scenario: I will flunk out of college, never get a job, and live in a cardboard box under a bridge. A quick reality check reveals that this is highly unlikely. You might get a B on your exam instead of an A. Not really life-threatening. But if you interpret it as such, you can plunge into fear and its debilitating effects.

Like astronaut Buzz Aldrin, some people can be at peace doing things that others would find stressful. Most humans, for example, would find diving into shark-infested waters quite threatening. Yet some people do this for fun. When I lived in Fiji, near my house there was a famous shark-diving expedition. A boat took diving enthusiasts to a shark haven where folks dove down and fed the massive creatures chunks of meat. The divemaster explained to me (on dry land—I don't pretend I did the dive, thank you very much) that sharks are quite friendly and rarely hurt people. He cited a statistic that more people are killed by cows every year than are killed by sharks. And more people in the state of New

York go to emergency rooms because they have been bitten by another person, than the number of people who are bitten by sharks around the entire planet. Danger lurks more in the fearful mind than in external circumstances. (Unless you live in New York and have a mate who likes to bite.)

Many of us have gotten so used to interpreting moderately challenging situations as life-threatening that we have become addicted to a certain level of adrenaline flowing through our system. If the adrenaline drops below a certain threshold, we get antsy and need to create another drama, thrill, or binge to feed the habit. This is one of the causes of adrenal fatigue. Some people would not know what to do without some drama going on. The ancient Greeks wisely invented the theatrical drama as an outlet to sublimate our fears so we are not shredded by them in real life. When we watch actors on a stage go through a crisis and resolve it, we vicariously purge our fear and feel relieved. We destress through fictitious characters, which are not so fictitious when we realize they represent parts of ourselves. This is why most stories have a happy ending, which gives us some comfort that our own challenges will somehow be resolved.

No Dramas, Mate

Is it possible to live without drama? Can we escape the stress that dramas induce? One day I had to pick up my lawnmower from a repair shop operated by an Australian guy. I was running late and phoned to tell him I might not get to the shop before it closed. "That's alright, mate," he replied with typical Aussie laid-back style. "No dramas." That was the first time I had heard that expression. In America we say, "no problem" or "no worries." "No dramas" took the concept to a whole new level.

We can de-dramatize our life and avoid the stress dramas induce by reinterpreting challenging situations when they arise. All of the voices we hear in our head can be boiled down to two: fear and love. Every thought, statement, feeling, and action proceeds from one or the other. When one of my coaching clients lays out a stressful problem, I ask, "What does the voice of fear tell you about this?" After the client expresses that voice, I ask, "What does the voice of love, trust, or confidence say about this?" When the client taps into the loving voice, I observe a marked change in her demeanor. The client's forehead smooths, her shoulders drop, she breathes more deeply, and her energy shifts from stress to ease. The stress that dramas cause is always fear-based. The path to resolving a scary drama is always love-based. As you practice reframing challenging situations to a broader, non-threatening context, you will defuse the drama in your life and clear the path to healing.

The Empty Emergency Room

A friend of mind serves as the information director for a hospital in Hawaii. She told me that when the coronavirus pandemic surged, the hospital's emergency room experienced its lowest usage in the history of the hospital. She explained this odd phenomenon with two reasons: First, Hawaii had one of the lowest incidences of coronavirus in the nation. Second—far more interesting—people chose not to come to the E.R. because they were afraid of getting Covid-19, and they had also been advised to leave room for expected coronavirus patients. "Lots of people who would have otherwise come in to be treated for sprained ankles, tweaked backs, or bruises from falls, chose to handle them at home or through alternative treatments," she explained.

Could many issues we would normally consider emergencies be treated at home? Would many ailments heal naturally without intervention if we just relaxed, rested, and took good care of ourselves? Might we avail ourselves of natural remedies that don't require a medical doctor's care?

I am not suggesting that you refrain from reaching out for medical care if you have a real emergency. Certain conditions require immediate attention by a qualified practitioner. If you need to go a doctor or the E.R., certainly go. But the Hawaii hospital's experience provides a telling clue that many situations we might normally consider to be an emergency, might be handled far more gently and easily, with less stress or drama.

The Line You Cannot Afford to Cross

When you enter a level of stress detrimental to your well-being, your body and emotions will give you clear signals that you have crossed a crucial line. You will experience specific symptoms that serve as red flags that you need to slow down, step back, and take another approach. You might get a sore throat, headache, indigestion, or skin rash. You may become irritable, demanding, or argumentative. You may get clumsy; drop, spill, break, or bump into things; make errors in your work; or have accidents. All of these manifestations generally do not occur when you are feeling good, healthy, relaxed, and on track with your passion and vision. They arise when you have overworked or gotten stressed or run down. While such symptoms may seem annoying or daunting, they are meaningful messages from the universe saying, "Stop, take a breath, and get your head on straight before you move ahead."

Yet instead of heeding the red flag, many people avoid, override, or numb the signals that have come to help them. They work harder; get busier; take a pill to mask the symptom; anaesthetize themselves with a drink, joint, television, web surfing, texting, or social media; or revert to a drug, gambling, meaningless sex, workaholism, obsessive cleaning, or other addiction. The ego is brilliant at drowning out the voice of love calling you to self-care. If you follow the ego, you may temporarily avoid the issue the signals are calling you to address, but eventually your body's natural homeostasis will get your attention. You may find yourself in bed, get sick, or face a difficult situation in your family, business, or relationships.

Take a moment now to consider:

What unique signs does your body give you,
letting you know that you that have crossed a crucial line?

What is your habitual response to those signs?

What can you do to respond more quickly,
healthfully, and effectively?

How can you engage in greater self-care
so you avoid a negative manifestation?

If you really loved yourself, what greater
kindnesses could you show yourself?

Most people in our culture would benefit from deeper self-care. More kindness to self, relaxation, slicing away toxic situations, and cultivating relationships with people we value would contribute immensely to undoing physical, mental, and emotional diseases at their core. You cannot err by being kinder to yourself. Many people feel guilty about doing good things for themselves because they have been taught that self-sacrifice is more valuable than self-nurturing. The opposite is true: When you are relaxed, happy, healthy, and creative, you are in the best position to make a positive contribution to your family, your community, and the world.

You do not have to become more blessed. You are already totally blessed. You just have to quit doing things that deny the blessings you already own. The fear-based ego will never admit your already-sufficiency; there is always one or many more things that have to happen before you can be fully blessed. When you find your soulmate, get that prestigious job, build your dream home, or win the lottery, then you will really be blessed. But, as you may have noticed, when one or all of those things happen, you find yourself reaching for the next thing that will make you *really* blessed. It's fine to reach for good things, but they will not fulfill you unless you find fulfillment right where you stand. The more you acknowledge the blessings you already own, the more blessings you will attract. We must proceed *from* blessings rather than reaching *toward* them.

Recognizing your blessings is the most effective stress management course you will ever find. God does not want you stressed or sick. Neither do you. Remove from your mind and experience any belief that stress serves you. There are easier ways to get where you need to go.

MASTER KEYS *of* THIS CHAPTER

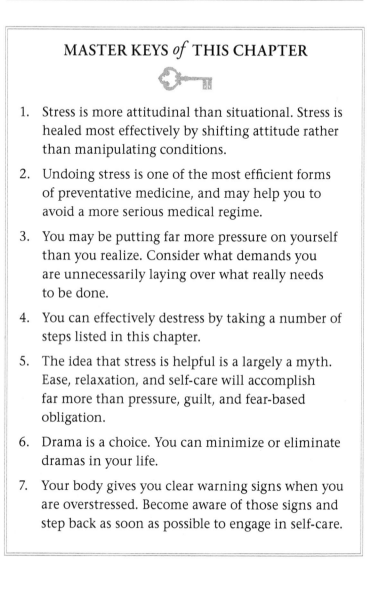

1. Stress is more attitudinal than situational. Stress is healed most effectively by shifting attitude rather than manipulating conditions.

2. Undoing stress is one of the most efficient forms of preventative medicine, and may help you to avoid a more serious medical regime.

3. You may be putting far more pressure on yourself than you realize. Consider what demands you are unnecessarily laying over what really needs to be done.

4. You can effectively destress by taking a number of steps listed in this chapter.

5. The idea that stress is helpful is a largely a myth. Ease, relaxation, and self-care will accomplish far more than pressure, guilt, and fear-based obligation.

6. Drama is a choice. You can minimize or eliminate dramas in your life.

7. Your body gives you clear warning signs when you are overstressed. Become aware of those signs and step back as soon as possible to engage in self-care.

MOBILIZING
PRAYER POWER

Sometimes all it takes is just one prayer
to change everything.

—SOURCE UNKNOWN

When I presented a seminar at the Four Seasons Maui, the manager told me that the hotel was sold out for the entire Christmas holiday season. Rooms at that facility go for anywhere from $500 per night for a basic room to $23,834 for the grand suite. I was amazed that so many people find so much money to fly to a luxury resort and immerse themselves in lavish amenities.

There is another kind of resort that is free, and restores us more deeply than an amenity-chocked hotel. Most people turn to prayer as a last resort. When all else fails, we pray. Yet if we resort to prayer as soon as a challenge arises, or keep our consciousness prayerful when no challenge arises, we save time and struggle and we manifest continual blessings. Prayer delivers our greatest power to heal because it lifts us above worldly sorrows and unites us with the Source of all well-being. It is our lifeline to all that is good. Prayer opens the door to grace, where the issues that trouble us are resolved by a love that embraces us in ways far beyond what the intellect can fathom.

Real prayer does not ask for healing; it accepts it. You do not have to *make* wellness happen; you just need to *let* it happen. At this moment God is sending you all the good you can imagine and far more, including perfect health. You just have to be a willing receiver.

Many people have a hard time accepting their blessings, including healing, because they hold erroneous beliefs about how to connect to the source of wellness. Jesus said, "You pray amiss." If you have a tool that can change your life, but you do not know how to use it, you are missing its immense benefit. Let us reverse that now. Here are some of the mistaken notions that stand between us and healing, and how to dissolve them:

1. The belief that God lives at a distance. We have been led to believe that God lives in some far distant heaven, with an untraversable gap between sinful, sorrowful humanity and the Source of our healing. We then conceive of prayer as a long-distance call to a father who has divorced himself from his family, and whom we must beg and plead for child support. But God has not deserted humanity. It is we who have turned our back on our Source. ("If you feel distant from God, who moved?") We can reconnect by recognizing that the divine presence is already here. The poet Kabir said, "I laugh when I hear that the fish in the water is thirsty." Alfred, Lord Tennyson said, "Closer is He than breathing, and nearer than hands and feet." When we understand that God is already with us, we don't have to struggle and sweat to reach Him. True prayer is a local call.

2. The belief that God is angry, vengeful, and finds value in our suffering. A *Course in Miracles* tells us that God's will for us is perfect happiness. The idea of a wrathful God is simply a projection of human vindictiveness. Voltaire noted, "God created us in His image and likeness, and we returned the compliment." Pray not to placate a punitive father, but to connect with the Father whose only desire is to give you the kingdom. God takes no delight in our pain, but wishes only for us to be healthy, prosperous, and in love. The purpose of prayer is to lift our thoughts and cleanse our vision so we see God as He is, not who we invented Him to be.

3. The belief that you must persuade God to dispense your good. You do not need to convince God to deliver your blessings. You must convince yourself to receive them. It is not God's mind you need to change, but your own. God has already made up His mind in our favor, and He is waiting for us to join Him. Theologian Phillips Brooks said, "Prayer is not the overcoming of God's reluctance, but the laying hold of God's willingness." If you believe that you have to fight, cajole, bargain, wheedle, or persuade God that you deserve blessings, you have dug yourself into a hole. God is already your greatest advocate and cheerleader for your health and prosperity. Spirit knows the immense good you deserve, and is eager to deliver it. God's prayer is that you catch up with the vision of you that He already holds. Thus we might regard prayer as the noblest exercise in self-esteem.

4. The belief that you are alone and helpless. In the visible world you have dear friends and family who love you, believe in you, want the best for you, and would do anything they can to help you. In the invisible world you have angels, guides, saints, ascended masters, and departed relatives who are rooting for you and can help you through flashes of inspiration, inner guidance, synchronistic events, connections with key people, and outright miracles. Your invisible friends are standing beside you at this moment, ready and able to pull strings on your behalf. Your part is to believe in them, ask for help, seize opportunities, and accept support when it shows up. It is said, "When you work, God rests. When you rest, God works." This does not mean you cease to act, or be lazy. It means you can quit trying to do it all by yourself, and let Higher Power help you.

5. The belief that you are allowed just so much good. My client Marcie told me that doctors had once declared her infertile and predicted she would never have a child. Then she and her husband prayed for a child and she miraculously conceived and gave birth. Now the couple wants another child and hasn't been able to get pregnant. "Do you think I used up all my miracles on that first child?" she asked me. Her question demonstrates the belief that we deserve just so much good and no more. I told her that the God who granted her prayers for one child is perfectly capable of granting prayers for more children. This woman was not bumping up against limitations set by God, but the limitations of her own beliefs. Her parenting journey is not just about bringing children into the world, but about learning that God does not meter out blessings and miracles like poor parents who ration a limited food supply to their children. The universe is limitless in its ability to give us all we need. We just need to let it in. I know many people who were told they would never be healed, and they were. There are higher laws than science understands.

6. The belief that it is selfish to ask for material things. God wants you to have all you need in the material world. Don't deny yourself physical things that would make your life easier; to accept them is a form of receiving God's love. The Urtext version of *A Course in Miracles* records a conversation between Jesus, who authored the Course, and Helen Schucman, who scribed it. Helen had been looking to buy a winter coat at a luxury department store, but Jesus specifically guided her to find the same coat at another store at a less expensive price. At that store Helen met a salesman who needed advice for his disabled child. As a psychologist who specialized in that type of disability, Helen was able to help him. So there was a deeper purpose to the guidance Helen received. She got the coat and also delivered a blessing.

7. The belief that you must pray in a particular way. If you were raised in a religion that prescribes certain rote prayers, and taught that in order to get God's attention you must pray those prayers, you may avoid praying altogether and miss out on its benefits. You might also carry painful memories of hearing a preacher trying to scare you with threats of hell, or sitting amidst a large congregation muttering spiritless words, their minds straying to the golf course or Sunday brunch. If you are turned off to traditional prayers, feel free to formulate your own. God does not hear the words we pray, but the sincerity and intention behind them. One heartfelt word motivated by a true desire to connect with God is more powerful than a thousand hollow words. Jesus urged us to avoid vain repetition. If you like traditional prayers and find them uplifting, carry on. If you prefer to simply speak from your heart to the God you most comfortably relate to, you are good to go.

Gratitude, the Master Prayer

While most people pray asking for things, a smaller number pray thanking for things. Prayers of gratitude are more powerful than prayers of asking because gratitude represents the recognition of the presence and benevolence of God, which is the deeper purpose of prayer.

Giving thanks for the good we have attracts more good to us. Dwelling on blessings leads us to more blessings, and dwelling on complaints leads us to more complaints. The mind operates on scientific principles. By analogy, your car is a neutral machine without independent volition. It will go wherever you drive it. You can cruise along a superhighway or run your vehicle into a ditch. So it is with your mind. It will follow your lead and manifest results according to thoughts you use to steer it.

One of the most powerful ways to accelerate healing is to be thankful for the health you have. Complaining about what you are missing won't take you where you want to go. I heard about an amateur pilot whose small airplane crashed when he flew it into utility wires on his approach to land. The pilot survived, but he remained mostly paralyzed. The only part of his body he could move was the little finger on one hand. For weeks he lay in a hospital bed, depressed about his predicament. Then he decided to be grateful for the capacity he had, little though it was. He began to use his little finger to communicate, making signals for yes and no, and pointing to letters on an alphabet board that helped him converse with his family and visitors. When he moved into appreciation for this faculty, he regained use of another finger, and was thrilled to expand his repertoire. Then he could move another finger, and another, all the while giving thanks for more agility. Eventually he regained use of his entire body. The turning point came when he ceased to be despondent about what he couldn't do, and celebrated what he could do.

Gratitude is the most powerful prayer, as it lifts us to our natural state of love. Even if you didn't believe in God or a spiritual reality, and you lived a life filled with gratitude, you would be very close to God. You are already very close to God, and prayers of appreciation remind of us of our inherently exalted state.

Pray Your Way through Your Day

It is very helpful to have a regular prayer practice. When you begin each day by spending quality time with God, you set your mind up to receive good throughout your day. Pray your way into your day before you get involved in the world's details. If the first thing you do when you wake up is finger your phone, your phone has become your god. If you turn on the news before you get out of bed, you are worshiping at the altar of fear. Psychologists tell us that the first five years of a child's life are the formative years, which etch the patterns of that person's psyche for her entire life. Likewise, the first five minutes (or twenty minutes of prayer, let's say) are the formative minutes of your day. When you start your day connected to Higher Power, you set yourself up to remain connected. Such an investment yields returns far beyond the time you put in.

If at any point during your day you become distracted, upset, or fatigued, return to prayer. Step away from your desk, take some deep breaths, creatively visualize, sit in the sun, take a walk, or do whatever you need to reestablish your connection. A few minutes of focused positive thought can achieve a crucial course correction, a pivotal reset that will make you feel as if you are starting your day anew.

Another important time to connect with Spirit is just before you go to sleep. If you end your day watching news or a dramatic, action, or horror movie, you will need to work out the negativity in your dream world. Take some quiet time to segue from the activities of your day to your time of slumber. Prayer will quiet your mind and lead you to deep sleep. When you have nightmares, you are processing unresolved emotional experiences from your day. Praying before retiring will accomplish that important cleansing. Ask for a good night's sleep and invite your guides and angels to deliver any messages that can help you. You will sleep well, need to sleep less, and awaken refreshed, renewed, and healed.

If you prefer to meditate rather than pray, that works too. Meditation is a form of prayer in that it takes you to the quiet place where the raucous rants of the monkey mind are silenced. When the mind is quiet, you come into alignment with Spirit. When you quit listening to the ego's voice, you will hear God's voice. If you wish, complete your meditation period with some prayer. Buddhists speak a lovely blessing: "May all beings be free of suffering. May all beings be happy." When you pray for others, you not only help them; you lift your mind to a healing consciousness, which spills its blessings to you, as well. Any practice that lifts your mind and heart above worldly troubles, and regards you and others as embraced by the divine, is a valid prayer.

You have a real relationship with God, even if you don't call it that. Prayer is our most powerful tool to return to our natural state of wellness. In the beloved movie, E.T. kept asking to "phone home," symbolizing that we all need to connect with our home. Like E.T., you are just visiting this planet. Your true home is in Spirit. Prayer, in whatever form works for you, is the missing link between your life on earth and your home in God. You've used the first portion of your round-trip ticket from heaven to earth; prayer is your ticket home.

MASTER KEYS *of* THIS CHAPTER

1. Prayer provides our greatest power to heal because it lifts us above worldly sorrows and unites us with the Source of well-being.

2. While most people turn to prayer as a last resort, if we turn to prayer immediately when challenged, and maintain a prayerful attitude, we won't have to reach a dire situation.

3. Many people pray amiss. Study this chapter's list of illusions about prayer and the truths that offset them, and you will amplify your prayer power and its results.

4. Gratitude is the most powerful prayer, as it acknowledges the blessings you have already received, and opens the door for more.

5. Maintain a prayerful state of mind throughout the day. Begin and end your day with prayer. If during the day you feel distracted from peace, step back and pray to restore your right mind.

6. Meditation, affirmation, visualization, and joyful activities are valid forms of prayer. Any practice that connects you to the mind and heart of God is an act of prayer.

VISIONARY HEALING

Doctors don't know everything really.
They understand matter, not spirit.
And you and I live in the spirit.

—WILLIAM SAROYAN

True healers are visionaries. They are not distracted by the symptoms the body presents. They recognize that the patient's divine nature remains fully intact, undiminishable by physical maladies. Healers establish themselves at a higher frequency and invite patients to meet them there. When Jesus was asked to come to the home of a little girl whose parents reported her dead, he stated firmly, "The girl is not dead. She is just sleeping." He sat at the girl's bedside, spoke a few potent words, and the child was restored. Later the master arrived at the cave where Lazarus had been entombed for four days. Jesus stood before the sepulcher and commanded, "Lazarus, come forth!" Moments later Lazarus appeared, life animating him once again. The key question is, "to whom was Jesus speaking?" Was he speaking to the Lazarus who lay decaying, irretrievable to his mourning family? Or was he speaking to the Lazarus who thrived in a dimension imperceptible to the physical senses? Jesus had to be addressing the eternal, immortal, inviolate spirit Lazarus, not subject to the corruption of the flesh. Jesus knew precisely who Lazarus was, and he was not deterred by people who saw him as less.

If you wish to heal or be healed, immerse your mind in perfection rather than corruption. Do not restrict your vision to the body only. Give your attention to the radiant self unafflicted by symptoms. Do not see illness, but health. Do not see frailty, but strength. Do not see brokenness, but wholeness. Establish yourself in the lofty reality in which Jesus and other great healers dwell, and you will reap the results they have begotten.

When Hell becomes Heaven

When I volunteered to teach yoga in the veteran's hospital I mentioned, I was quite distraught to find all of the patients bound in wheelchairs. Some were amputees, many decrepit, and others depressed. I was put off by the odor from their diapers. Their sad predicament was aggravated by the fact that the hospital was understaffed, and the doctors and nurses had to split their attention among a large population. I had never seen such misery in my life; I felt like Prince Siddhartha, who grew up in a sheltered castle and then discovered that illness, old age, and death surrounded his pampered enclave.

I felt so daunted by this sorrowful scenario that when the time came for me to teach the third week's class, I forgot to go; that was the depth of my resistance. When I realized I was allowing fear to stop me, I introspected deeply to see if there was any way I could continue. I decided to go back and not focus on the patients' infirmities, but instead see them as shining spirits, independent of their physical limitations. I would connect with them at a heart level, and enjoy them as they were, rather than feel sorry for what they weren't.

The results of my shifted attitude were phenomenal! The patients enjoyed the class, joking and laughing. I went on to lead the patients in stirring guided visualizations. One day I asked them to see themselves as nineteen years old, running on a beach at sunset. As I was leading the imagery, a voice inside my head chided me, "You are so cruel! These poor people can't even walk, and you are reminding them that they will never walk, let alone run on the beach, or anywhere, ever again." But when I looked around the room, faces were smiling. Some had tears of joy. They loved the exercise, thanked me for it, and later often asked me to repeat it.

I realized that I was one of the few people in that hospital who saw those patients as greater than their afflictions. I pierced beyond the fettered senses and treated them as glowing spirits. The patients caught my vision and felt affirmed and uplifted.

Over time my class became the most popular in the hospital. Each week a long line of patients in wheelchairs queued up far down the hallway waiting to get in, reminiscent of the endless ribbon of cars at the conclusion of the movie *Field of Dreams*, on their way to visit the fabled baseball field once the object of folly, now a portal to soul renewal. The hospital meeting room was packed, and I had many regular attendees with whom I developed rewarding relationships. I came to adore those people who had at first frightened me. I taught those classes for seven years, and when I moved away from the area, one of my evening school yoga students took over. That room was transformed from a pit of hell to the heights of heaven—all starting with a simple shift of vision.

Clearing Your Sight

You don't see yourself as you are, or others as they are. You see a version of who you are, a densely veiled and highly distorted image tainted by years of cultural conditioning by people who projected their sense of limitation onto you. When you look upon others, you see their bodies, personalities, history, labels, and your judgments about them. If you saw yourself and others clearly, you would see only blazing light, and you would dwell in constant love. To see through the eyes of love is to see truly.

The people who love you see your true self. They do not participate in dark opinions, including your own. Real friends recognize that you are far more than your physical attributes, character flaws, and mistakes. "A friend is someone who sees through you and enjoys the view." Your essence is holy; all else is detail and passing appearances. When you know this, shortsighted vision gives way to the redeeming big picture.

Likewise, your greatest gift to your friends and clients is your highest vision of them. The purpose of relationship is to bring out the best in each other. If you are fanning the flame of magnificence in your marriage, family, and close connections, you are fulfilling your relationship destiny. If you are focusing on flaws and faults, you are reinforcing error and illusion. The appearance of pain and limits signals a call to upgrade your vision. Healed vision leads to healed relationships, which leads to healed bodies. The darker or more painful the relationship, the greater the release, relief, and reward when the relationship is restored to its natural state. *A Course in Miracles* tells us, "The holiest spot on earth is where an ancient hatred has become a present love."

The Quest of a Lifetime

Discovering your true self is the quest of a lifetime, your most compelling purpose. When you know who you are, you know who everyone else is—an expression of God breathed into the world, to be discovered, unfolded, and celebrated. True vision soars beyond the paltry gifts the world pursues, and unveils the jewel of great price. The most valuable diamond in the world is worthless compared to your true self. All of your experiences, over one lifetime or many, lead to self-recognition. There is no other reason for anything that happens to you.

Your highest calling is to affirm your true identity, and that of others, in situations the world encumbers with limited sight. It's easy to see the best in yourself and others when they are kind and loving to you. The greater opportunity is to see the best in them when they are withholding their love and acting in unkind ways. Your quest is not to set things right, but to see them rightly. Such elevated vision will set in motion a wave of healing that diminished vision can never accomplish.

While you may believe your job is to fix a troubled person or their situation, your deeper task is to change your mind about who that person is. Help them logistically where you can, but maintain your knowing of their best self. To see your friend or patient as lacking, broken, or victimized only keeps that person bound, along with you. Your gift to that person is your gift yourself. When you recognize that both of you are whole, empowered, and capable, you are liberated. You do not have to lay on hands, wave a crystal, or utter a prayer or incantation to heal, although you can certainly do so if you find such methods helpful. More fundamentally, maintain your vision of wellness rather than disease. To be more, you must see more.

After establishing himself over many years as a world-renowned transformer of consciousness, Ram Dass had a stroke, after which he was confined to a wheelchair and dealt with various physical ailments. In spite of his bodily challenges, Ram Dass maintained an attitude of immense joy, love, lightheartedness, and connection to Spirit until his passing at age 88. Right until the time of his passing, he taught often and enthusiastically, and lit up the room with his smile and presence. If ever there was a living demonstration that our true self transcends the body, it was Ram Dass. Dass, who blesses us now from a higher dimension.

During one of my seminars with Ram Dass, for a moment I played devil's advocate: "What would you say to a person who argues, 'There is so much pain, suffering, and loss in the world. How can I possibly be happy and healthy amidst such a dismal state of affairs?'"

Ram Dass thought for a moment, smiled, and replied, "Change your mind."

It is seductive to believe that we must change the world before we can be at peace. Yet it is precisely in coming to peace that we gain our greatest power to change the world. Manipulating the mind yields far more potent results than manipulating conditions. Only from an upgrade of vision is a lasting change in conditions possible. When we move the spotlight from the outer to the inner, the path to healing becomes clear, including any actions we can take on our behalf or others'. When you recognize that how you see the world is the strongest factor in improving the world, the sacred power to which all great healers have access is yours.

If you feel like you don't fit into the world you inherited
it is because you were born to help create a new one.

—Ross Caligiuri

MASTER KEYS *of* THIS CHAPTER

1. Authentic healers are visionaries. They see beyond material conditions or symptoms, into a perfect spiritual reality.

2. When you see people as frail, broken, or helpless, you reinforce that experience for them and yourself. When you see them as whole, strong, and empowered, you lift them to that experience, as well as yourself.

3. Bodies, personalities, histories, and judgments distract us from seeing ourselves and each other clearly. We see *our versions* of each other, not our souls. Real healing is founded in soul recognition.

4. The people who love you see your true self. They are not fooled by your errors or supposed sins. To truly love others, see their true self.

5. The greater the pain or interpersonal conflict, the greater the release and expansion of light when it is healed. "The holiest spot on earth is where an ancient hatred has become a present love."

6. Self-discovery is your deepest purpose, as it is for your patients and loved ones. When you know who you are, your vision becomes clear and you know what you are here to do.

7. Real spiritual mastery is attained by a change of mind more than manipulating conditions. When mind changes, conditions follow.

WHAT WILL YOU DO
WITH YOUR HEALING?

As we express our gratitude, we must never
forget that the highest appreciation is not
to utter words but to live by them.

–JOHN F. KENNEDY

Every day a stream of people showed up at Hilda Charl-ton's Manhattan apartment, seeking relief from their physical, emotional, financial, and relationship problems. Hilda was a rare soul with a constant connection to Source. Many people were healed and experienced profound life changes as a result of her positive influence.

One day I heard Hilda counseling a woman who came to her for prayer for physical healing. "What will you do with your life if you get your health back?" Hilda asked the woman.

It didn't take long for the lady to answer. "I will take good care of myself and help make others' lives easier."

Hilda smiled and went on to pray to restore the woman's wellness.

Now, many years later, I more fully appreciate Hilda's question. Many people don't appreciate their health until they start to lose it. Then they think about why they are here, what is important, and how to make the most of their time on Earth. If someone's unconscious or self-defeating behavior leads to an illness and they get healed, but they continue with negative habits, the illness has not served. If the person's body is restored to functionality but their mind remains mired in fear or illusion, we cannot say they were truly healed. The person will likely face a recurrence of the issue or encounter a different one until they heed the wake-up call. But we don't need to get sick to consider and upgrade the quality of our thoughts and life. A person in her right mind will strive to live at the highest octave rather than waiting for pain to sound an alarm. Yet many of us are stubborn when it comes to changing our life. Sometimes it takes a two-by-four to get our attention.

Physical health or the manifestation of a material blessing is not the end goal of the healing process; it is but an intermediate step in the transformation of the mind. If you get healed, find your soulmate, or move into your dream home, but do not recognize the presence of a Higher Power as the Source of your manifestation, and your mind remains in the same condition it was before your prayer was answered, you have not taken the most important step. While Bruno Gröning delivered physical healing to many thousands of people, he stated that his ultimate purpose was to help them find their way back to God. Every experience leads to the recognition of the divine. When that occurs, the entire journey makes sense, and we understand the challenges as steppingstones toward home.

The Hero's Gift

Many people who experience a healing are moved to help others who face the same difficulty. Esteemed mythologist Joseph Campbell mapped what he called "the hero's journey," in which we grow through overcoming a challenge. Ultimately the hero—each of us—returns with a gift. We see, know, or feel something we did not perceive before the adventure began. Then we pass along what we have learned and guide others to improve their lives as we have improved ours. Thus we complete the sacred cycle.

People who have mastered a particular challenge are the most qualified to teach that lesson. Those who have gone through alcoholism are in the perfect position to sponsor individuals struggling with the addiction. Those who have lost weight are qualified to teach others to lighten up. People who have found their way out of abusive situations can map the route for others to free themselves.

Such wayshowers do not simply find satisfaction in helping others; through their teaching they strengthen themselves. The healing we give passes through us, so we receive the benefit along with our friend or patient. In the famous healer's prayer in *A Course in Miracles,* we are asked to affirm, "I will be healed as I let Him teach me to heal." I like to paraphrase, "I will be healed as I allow Him to heal through me." Genuine healing is never just for the recipient; the healer receives what she gives.

Take Care Who You Tell

After Jesus healed a leper, he told him, "Do not tell anyone." This directive may sound odd, as we might expect Jesus to advise the man to make a public testimony to celebrate the healing, give credit to God, and inspire others to be healed. But in this case we learn from Jesus the metaphysician more than the religious icon. The master healer was also a master psychologist who understood the dynamics of how the human mind works. The healed leper needed to concretize his healing within his own mind before he announced it to the world.

Likewise, if you broadcast a healing or positive event soon after it happens, you may incur judgment or resistance from others. The critical mind is vicious when it comes to events it cannot understand; it will tear to shreds what doesn't fit into its limited belief system. Jesus also directed, "Don't cast pearls before swine." The swine is the fearful, malicious, jealous ego that cannot stand to see someone else succeed. Misery is threatened by joy, and it will do all it can to keep shards of light from penetrating its fortified dungeon. "That's just your imagination," someone says when hearing about your healing. "You're being naïve—get real." "I know someone who had a healing like that and the disease came back." I was visiting a young woman in the hospital who had just had a very minor surgery. I heard a relative at her bedside tell her, "I know someone who died from that." I couldn't believe that someone would lay such a dire statement on someone trying to heal! Maybe that's why "friends are God's way of apologizing for your relatives."

If your healing is fresh and tender and you are still wrapping your mind around it, adverse comments can shake your confidence or set your recovery back. Until your healing is gelled in your experience, you do better to not speak of it or speak of it only to people you know will support you. Yogis offer the analogy of a seedling planted in a field where cattle graze. If you leave the little tree unprotected, the cattle will trample or eat it. You must build a fence around the sapling to protect it while it is developing. After it grows to become substantial and sturdy, you can remove the fence, and one day the tree will be so tall and strong that the cattle can rub up against it and rest in its shade. My mentor likened a healing or new awareness to an embryo in the womb. "You don't let anyone poke at it," she said. She later gave a stronger analogy: "Don't skydive while you're pregnant."

At the deepest level, no one has the power to ruin your healing or project. But until your mind is firm about the experience, you may ascribe that power to them. So Jesus' advice to the healed man was not so much a comment about other people as it was about the man's mind and, ultimately, ours.

Don't Try to Heal What's Already Healed

At the end of each of her classes, Hilda performed healing treatments on students, through prayer, affirmation, and laying on of hands. One night she worked intently on a young woman who had been in a lot of pain, and then reported she felt a lot better after Hilda's treatment.

At the following week's class, Hilda admonished the students. "Last week after I healed a girl, on her way out of the class someone told her, 'I can recommend some herbs that will heal you.' Why would you recommend a healing treatment to someone who was healed? When you do that, you affirm that she is sick and needs healing. Don't undo my healing. If someone is healed, treat them as such."

Hilda was offering an advanced lesson in how to maintain a healing consciousness and support others to do the same. You are either healed or you are not. If you are healed, you are on one path. If you are not healed, you are on another path. Healing and illness function at two entirely different frequencies. If you are on the healing frequency, don't lower your frequency and do things that someone still needing healing would do.

This lesson is for those who have strong faith and recognize the power of the mind. If, after you receive a healing treatment, you still feel you need herbs, drugs, or some other treatment, go ahead. Use the permission slip you believe in. If you don't have faith in the healing you have received, go where your faith lives. Hilda's lesson functions on a more subtle plane. It is ultimately the purest and most effective level of healing because it heals at the level of the mind, the source of all illness and healing, not simply at the level of symptoms or external manipulation.

Chutes and Ladders

The ego does not relinquish its grip gracefully or quickly. It will use every trick at its disposal to cling to its throne of power and control your life. If you have experienced a healing, you may face various temptations that cause you to backslide or misuse the gift you have received. Here are a few of the most common chutes, along with the ladders that take us back to higher elevations:

1. You grow complacent. As you start to feel better, you slip back into old habits that contributed to the disease. You may think, "I'm better now. I can do what I want." You might revert to an unhealthy diet, laziness, overworking, putting yourself in stressful situations, hanging out in toxic environments, associating with negative people, indulging fear-based or self-defeating thoughts and behaviors, or other diversions. If you find yourself falling into such a rut, return to humility. Appreciate that your healing was a gift from God, and do your part to maintain it. Don't take healing for granted. There was a lesson attached to regaining your health. Keep making that lesson work on your behalf.

2. You forget the Source of your healing. When we get into trouble, we call on God. "There are no atheists in a foxhole."

When we get out of trouble, we may forget the Source of our good. In the movie *The Longest Yard*, Paul Crewe tries to drown himself out in the ocean, but then changes his mind. As he struggles to swim back to shore, he negotiates with the Lord. "If you save my life, I'll give you fifty percent of my income." Then, as he gets closer to shore, he lowers the percentage. When he finally reaches land, he says, "Okay, the ten percent is yours—if you want it." Paul stands on solid ground and, instead of thanking God for saving him, he blames God, "You were the one who made me sick."

When Paul was in danger, he realized he needed help from a Higher Power. When he was out of danger, he denied Higher Power. None of us are capable to sustain ourselves. We are sustained only by God. You do not know how to keep your heart beating, your lungs breathing, or how to ensure your food supply. You participate and cooperate with those processes, but ultimately you live by Grace. If you think you are doing it all by yourself, you will feel separate from God and miss the Source and experience of your blessings.

We did not create ourselves and we do not sustain ourselves. We are dependent on the love of God for all of our good. Fortunately, that love is constant and unconditional. Let us always give credit where credit is due. Humility is a virtue of the highest empowerment.

3. You develop an identity around your disease. My friend Peter had bouts with severe depression for many years. Then he discovered a method that helped him work his way out of the rut, and he became a far happier and healthier person. As a result, Peter gave lectures on overcoming depression, wrote a book on the subject, and attained considerable success. I attended some of Peter's lectures, which were inspiring and helpful to his audience. As I heard Peter tell the same depression story over and over and over again, I thought, "If that were me, I would get depressed talking end-lessly about my depression." His talks revealed his healing strategy, but I personally would not want to continually go over the same story or be known as "the depression guy." I suggested to Peter that he might want to tweak his brand-ing so he could talk about something else and develop a more expanded identity. While overcoming depression was a significant milestone on his spiritual journey, he is a dif-ferent person now. Why not identify with who you have become rather than who you were? It is tempting to cling to an old identity, especially if you are reaping a profit from it. But stepping into a new and greater self-image is far more profitable. When I later saw Peter, he told me that he had expanded his subject matter and he was enjoying teaching a lot more.

4. *You get distracted.* If you become identified as a healed person or a healer, you may be sidetracked by various allures like money, power, fame, or sex. People seeking healing may adore you, throw themselves at you, or become dependent on you. They may identify you as the source of their salva-tion. If you are not careful, you may accept that danger-laden role. Or you might develop a product, business, or career around your story or your method of healing, all of which is fine as long as the business does not own you. Some healers get so involved in their healing-related business that they lose sight of the Power and principles that got them healed. They get busy, stressed, greedy, sexually involved with con-stituents, enmeshed in legal issues, or become so consumed with a world salvation mission that they lose their peace. When you lose your peace, you are no longer healed. At such a point you must stop and do whatever it takes to regain your healed mind and body.

Jesus said, "enter by the narrow gate," meaning that to get and stay healed you must be absolutely committed to healing and not fall off the path, which can easily happen if you're not careful. Don't let the ego's endless bag of tricks lure you from well-being. If you find that you have become distracted, be honest and return to your path as quickly as possible. Keep choosing what got you healed.

5. You do not discern between healthy and unhealthy influences and associations. People who become well-known healers or teachers are vulnerable to individuals seeking to exploit them. Seedy characters see the healer as a cash cow and, under the guise of helping them develop their ministry or business, milk them for personal profit. Edgar Cayce is one of the best-known healers in the world. While in trance, Cayce gave thousands of readings with uncanny accuracy and suggested holistic remedies that helped many people regain their health. But, like many gifted visionaries, he was not deft at navigating earthly matters, especially the world of finance. As a result, he attracted people who bilked him for his income, and in spite of the huge gifts he brought to the world, he struggled with money continuously. Bruno Gröning was subject to similar dark influences in the form of people who offered to manage his healing service. While Gröning did not care about money and never charged a penny, his unethical managers charged people for the privilege to see Gröning, and pocketed large sums of cash for themselves. If you get healed and wish to pass your technique or services along to others, be smart about money and don't allow unscrupulous people to take advantage of you or your clients.

6. You proselytize. Proselytizing is born of insecurity. Only the ego requires people to join or follow you in order to validate your beliefs. Spiritual truth is not measured by numbers of bodies, but by the quality of experience. If you need people to do what you do, your healing is not complete. You may have healed your body, but not your mind. If one or many people wish to share your path, that's wonderful. If no one does, that's fine too. The ego seeks allies; the spirit seeks peers. When you make a clear statement about who you are and what you believe, those who recognize and match you will walk by your side. These are the people who matter. Better to join with a smaller number of people who are aligned with your vision than a larger number who are not. If a larger number show up, guided by Spirit, then that is the ministry to which you are assigned. I love the twelve-step tradition, "Our public relations policy is based on attraction rather than promotion." Your positive energy and integrity will naturally convince and convert. Healing speaks for itself. Don't interrupt it by trying to sell others on it. Real healing is contagious. Those who need it catch it from those who have it. Transform with your being more than your words.

7. You become a vengeful crusader. To be right, you don't have to make anyone wrong. Simply stand for what you believe in. To champion holistic healing, you don't have to attack allopathic medicine. To encourage vegetarianism, you don't have to slam meat eaters or producers. If you want to advance racial or gender equality, don't hate those who aren't there yet. Being a proponent does not require you to be an opponent. Certainly you can educate others as to the problems you wish to eradicate and point out what is not working in a dysfunctional system. Many world change agents have exposed ills that have, as a result, been corrected. The question is, "Are you motivated by your vision for positive change, or are you seething with anger against what you oppose?" There is nothing more oxymoronic than a militant vegetarian. Confucius warned, "Before you embark on a journey of revenge, dig two graves." Mature transformers stay focused on where we are going more than where we are coming from. Martin Luther King, Jr.'s classic speech was titled, "I Have a Dream," not "We Have a Nightmare." He stated, "You have very little morally persuasive power with people who can feel your underlying contempt."

There is only one thing you must do with a healed life: live it. Experience, exemplify, and model your healing. Stay in the mind-set of well-being. Healing is not a one-time event, but an ongoing process. It is not simply an ending to disease, but the beginning of a new pattern of life. If God heals you, do your part to maintain your healing. God's faith in you calls for your faith in Spirit and yourself. Remember where you came from and use your healing to keep your life better and help others make their lives better. Healing restores you to your natural state. Build your house there and dwell in it gratefully.

MASTER KEYS *of* THIS CHAPTER

1. One purpose of healing is to establish a course correction that improves the quality of the patient's life.

2. If the patient continues the same habits, patterns, or state of mind that led to the illness, the healing has not served its highest purpose.

3. If symptoms are removed but the client does not improve his attitude or lifestyle, the symptoms will likely recur.

4. The best healers use physical healing as a springboard to stimulate the patient's spiritual growth.

5. People who have experienced a healing and the soul growth that comes from it are called to pass their learning along to others. Such people are the most qualified to help those who are going through a similar challenge.

6. If you publicly acknowledge a healing while it is new and tender, you may encounter resistance and negativity from others that may set your healing back. Better to not speak of the healing publicly until it is firmly established, or speak of it only to people who support you.

7. If someone has experienced a healing, don't treat them as if they are not healed, by recommending further healing treatments.

8. You can avoid or offset the errors that some people make after a healing, by using the remedies listed in this chapter.

The
HEALED
HEALER

THE WOUNDED HEALER

*Only the wounded healer is able to heal. As long
as we think that spiritual leaders need to be perfect,
we live in poverty. I have a perfect teacher inside;
there is no perfect teacher outside.*

—ANGEL WILLIAMS

I sat in the green room backstage at a large motivational
conference, chatting with some of the other teachers.
Meanwhile a world-famous author delivered the keynote
lecture to a group of 3,000 avid fans who had traveled from
far and wide to learn from him and other presenters on
the theme, "The Keys to Happiness." Finally a thunderous
ovation from the ballroom signaled that the speaker had
completed the address. A minute later he strode into the
green room looking relieved. He plopped down on a couch,
grabbed a bottle of water, and confessed, "I don't know how
I gave that lecture. I haven't been happy a day in my life."

While it appears that teachers, healers, and leaders have
their lives together, they struggle with the same conflicts
and challenges that you and I face in our relationships,
finances, careers, and health. It is tempting to iconize self-
help, motivational, and inspirational teachers, bestowing
them the status of gods. Meanwhile they, like all of us, are
human beings on a learning curve of awakening. While we
can benefit from their profound insights, we can also learn

from their challenges and, more importantly, how they deal with them.

I have put spiritual celebrities on a pedestal, at the expense of acknowledging their human foibles. When I eventually observed their character deficits, I felt disillusioned. How could that person live in a way that contradicts their message? Like the bestselling inspirational author who hired a prostitute to come to his hotel room, and the woman mistakenly went to the conference organizer's room and explained she was looking for the keynoter to deliver her services; or the channeler who did not show up for her lecture, and when the team leader went to her room to check on her, found her dead drunk; or the minister of a large church who was asked to resign because he was sleeping with the wife of one of the board members; or the "how to stop smoking" teacher observed smoking in the alleyway during a class break; or the authority on vegan nutrition who was photographed digging into a Texas barbeque.

In this chapter we will examine how to relate to healers who do not walk their talk, and how to reframe their deficits, as well as our own, so they become assets. My purpose is not to discredit or disparage any teacher, all of whom deliver significant gifts and uplift the lives of many. To the contrary, I wish to: (1) demonstrate that healers, like all of us, embody both strengths and weaknesses; (2) learn from their mistakes; (3) gain compassion for their shortcomings and our own; and (4) demonstrate how good teachers grow through their challenges and pass their insights and victories along to help others.

I also wish for you to recognize that you are capable to teach and heal even if you are not perfect. Many of us have a tendency to compare ourselves to teachers we admire, believing they are closer to God than we are. Then we judge ourselves for coming up short. Such nearsighted adoration casts us into the jaws of judgment and justifies our hiding in the shadows, our gifts undelivered. When we realize that even great healers and teachers struggle with the same kinds of issues we face, we erase our belief in hierarchy and recognize, "If that person can help others and attain success, so can I."

Neither do I purport to separate myself from the people and situations I mention. I certainly have my share of faults and shortcomings that keep me humbly on my learning curve. If you saw me in my moments of fear, upset, or unconscious behavior, you would recognize that we are all in the same boat. My spiritual path calls me to examine my own blind spots and learn to clear them. It is because I have wrestled with my own pain and faced my mistakes that I can teach about woundedness and illuminate the path to higher ground that I have discovered, often the hard way.

How to Deal with Discovering Faults in a Wounded Healer

While finding error or hypocrisy in someone you admire can be daunting, it can also be illuminating. Every experience, including disappointing ones, offers learning and healing. Here are some tips to turn observed minuses into pluses:

1. Take the healer off a pedestal. When you idolize a human being, you give your power away to that person. When you make that person more-than, you make yourself less-than. This is demeaning to yourself and undermines a healthy relationship. Plato said, "True friendship can occur only among equals." When you see yourself as one with a teacher, you erase superiority and inferiority, and you become a peer more than a fan. Certainly you can respect a teacher as a role model, but not at the expense of your own value and unique gifts.

2. Learn from that person's error. Everyone is your teacher. Some teach you what to do. Others teach you what not to do. Appreciate that person for walking ahead of you and taking on a challenge that helps you grow by observing how they handle it.

3. Respect honesty. If the teacher has voluntarily revealed her challenge, applaud her for being real about her process. If the teacher was exposed by one or more other persons, appreciate their willingness to come forth.

4. Have compassion for that person. People who do hurtful or unethical things are in pain. What fear or pain drove that person to act in that way? How would you like others to regard you if you acted unconsciously? Compassion does not mean that we condone unscrupulous or abusive behaviors. It means that we try to understand the source of that behavior so that we might improve on such a behavior in ourselves or help others do the same.

5. Take the best and leave the rest. Do not throw out the teacher's valid messages because of the invalid ones. If the greater part of a teacher's lessons or a healer's practices are helpful, focus on them rather than the lesser part. If we discounted every healer who made mistakes, we would have no healers to turn to.

6. Remember that the real healer is God. The person you call "healer" is a human being through which the real Healer does the work. Human beings are frail and fallible. Focus on God as the Source of the good that flows through that person, and pay less attention to the human personality. If you are discouraged when you observe faults in an adored teacher or yourself, you are being redirected to look inward and upward, from where all of our blessings come.

Honesty is Integrity

The mark of integrity is not how cool we look, but how honest we are about where we stand on our path of awakening. Teachers who are real about their humanity are the most compelling. At a conference, I sat on a panel with three well-known inspirational authors including Neale Donald Walsh, author of the popular *Conversations with God* series. The moderator asked each of us to answer the question, "What is it that most people don't know about you?" Neale took the microphone and answered, "Most people don't know that I don't always walk my talk." An awkward silence hung for a few moments, and then the audience burst into applause. Neale's honesty was disarming. You have to respect a guy who can be naked about his own process. No teacher walks their talk all the time; only a few will admit this. In stating that he doesn't always walk his talk, Neale *is* walking his talk by being authentic, which makes him a rare and outstanding teacher. A conversation with God does not have to be profoundly metaphysical. It can be humbly refreshing.

Meanwhile Use Discernment

Some healers have become corrupted to the point that their ego-driven behaviors dominate their teachings and eclipse the good work they set out to deliver. Some become lost in money and power trips; misuse clients for sexual gratification; egotistically assume messiah status; become embroiled in competition and possessiveness; or get involved in large-scale dramas that confuse and hurt many people. Such healers have seriously fallen off the path; they must be recognized as corrupt or deluded, and avoided. Yet they simultaneously serve as teachers of what not to do. We receive grace from their example, that we may learn to side-step their mistakes and maintain integrity on our own path.

While attempting to discern a healer's value can be confusing or daunting, you have a failsafe mechanism that answers your questions and guides your ship through fog or stormy seas. We all have an inner teacher—the real guru—that knows the difference between truth and illusion, and shows us what to believe and what to deny as false. When you become stuck or confused about a teacher or healer, go within and notice which teachings or treatments res-onate with you and which do not. Your inner guide will not fail you. When truth is spoken, you feel illuminated, inspired, and fulfilled. When truth is absent, you feel empty, confused, and soul-hungry. Whether you are a healer or a patient, speak and listen with your heart more than your mind. The mind is easily misled. Your heart remains con-nected to the heart of God. You know what you need to know when you need to know it.

The Message and the Messenger

You can receive a perfect message from an imperfect messenger. Don't confuse the two. Many wounded healers offer magnificent universal truths that can enlighten you and change your life. The fact that the messenger does not fully understand such truths or live them is less important than that you apply them and reap their benefit. Don't lose out on golden cargo because the delivery vehicle is dented. In a world of endless illusions, we must find truth wherever we can capture it, even in embers and glimmers. When a healer models his or her teachings, that is an ideal scenario. If they don't, don't let that stop you from learning and growing. Truth is like concentrated orange juice; you must add the water of practical application to make it useful. Even if a healer does not add water to concentrated teaching, you can add your own water, and enjoy the sweet benefits.

Pivot Power

There are two moments when a healed healer shines. The first is when the healer becomes so aligned with her spiritual source that the windows of heaven open up and the healer's God-given gifts pour through, delivering blessings to the client far beyond what the mundane world can conjure. The same dynamic applies to gifted artists, actors, dancers, musicians, speakers, and writers. When we observe someone tapping into inspired talent, we sit humbly in awe as God shows up on Earth through human expression. Such moments are the very best that life has to offer, when the veil between the physical and spiritual dissolves and we are lifted to the highest soul nurture of which a human being is capable.

The other moment at which a healed healer shines is when he makes a mistake, learns from it, and passes the awakening along to his clients or students, that they may grow through his experience. A spiritual master pivots on his missteps and models how you can do the same. A healer who acknowledges how he got from where he started to where he now stands, including his struggles, failures, and triumphs, is the most compelling teacher. Respect and learn from healers who use their humanity as a steppingstone to grow closer to divinity and guide you to do the same.

If you are a teacher, healer, or leader, be honest about your hardships as well as your successes. Students or patients cannot identify with a paragon. Sincere students want a teacher they can relate to, someone who has walked the same path they are walking. Be naked about your humanity while claiming your divinity. Both are elements in the spiritual journey we all share. As you demonstrate this skill, you will provide others with vision, inspiration, and tools to do the same.

One day we shall all walk free of wounds. Until then, let our suffering lead to our awakening.

MASTER KEYS *of* THIS CHAPTER

1. All healers have human flaws as well as divinely inspired gifts.

2. Don't discount the value of a healer's genuine healing just because you observe personality deficits.

3. If even great healers display human errors, you don't need to wait until you become perfect before you deliver your healing service.

4. Mature healers are open about the mistakes they have made, they learn from them, and pass along their lessons to their students and patients.

5. If you feel daunted when you discover that a healer is wounded, use the strategies listed in this chapter to make the best use of the experience and grow through it.

6. If a healer or an associated group is dysfunctional, unethical, or toxic, dissociate yourself from them.

7. Do not confuse the message with the messenger. You can learn from a wounded healer's teaching even if the healer does not practice what he or she teaches. It is *your* practice of the teachings that makes them valuable.

THE HEALED HEALER

Physician, heal thyself.

—LUKE 4:23

Patricia Sun is a gifted healer who has uplifted many lives. When her ex-husband had a stroke, she went to his hospital bedside and spent hours healing him. At one point a nurse asked Patricia, "What is your relationship to the patient?"

"I'm his ex-wife," she answered.

The nurse looked surprised. "We don't get many ex-spouses coming in to visit, let alone sit with a patient with the love you are displaying."

Patricia smiled. "We're not married anymore, but if I can help heal him, I will. Some things are more important than judgment and history."

Genuine healers serve not only through the life changes they stimulate in their patients, but also as role models that inspire us to cultivate noble qualities and skills in our own lives. These are the characteristics of a healed healer:

1. She acknowledges that she serves as a vehicle for a Higher Power working through her. Genuine healers do not take credit for their healing, but attribute it to universal life force available to all.

2. He places service before selfish interests, and seeks to help more than acquire money, power, ego, fame, or establish a personal empire.

3. She makes no distinctions between patients who are worthy of healing and those who are not. Religion, race, gender, age, culture, wealth, caste, nation, and personal history are irrelevant. If someone needs help and is willing to receive it, that person is worthy of treatment.

4. He is humbly honest about his own journey, reveals his humanity, and strives to stay on the leading edge of his own spiritual growth.

5. She does not compete with other healers, judge, or criticize those whose methods are different, or seek to be right by making others wrong.

6. He balances his work with self-renewal and soul nurturing. When stress arises, he steps back and takes care of himself so he doesn't burn out.

7. She does not proselytize, campaign to gather members, or evaluate her worth or success by a number of followers. She trusts the law of attraction to join her with the people she can most help, be they few or many.

8. He is willing to flow and evolve in the techniques he subscribes to, open to changing and expanding, and lets go of old smaller beliefs to embrace new and greater ones.

9. She respects the rights of patients to choose healing or not, recognizing that her patients have their own learning curve and they will come to healing in their own right way and timing.

10. He establishes his vision in the wholeness and wellness of his patients, and does not label or join them in their sense of limitation. He does not seek to magnify their sense of need, but decreases it. His goal is to support clients to be independent of treatment.

Healers Worth Learning From

Many great healers have walked the Earth. Some are well known, and others have flown under the radar. I will note here a few of the healers who have affected me most profoundly, highlighting their gifts that have educated and inspired me, and will hopefully illuminate your journey as well.

Jesus Christ recognized his oneness with God and calls to us to join him as a peer. He refused to succumb to the small-mindedness of the religious leaders of his time, who supposedly represented God but were severely distracted from truth. He overturned tradition and karma in favor of compassion and grace. He remained established in the law of love and kept kindness as his highest priority. Christ could heal the sick and raise the dead because he knew that wellness and life are the will of God. He was clear on his spiritual lineage and urges us to share his divine identity. He was willing to put his body aside to demonstrate that we are all more than our bodies. Christ's healing power continues to ripple through the universe, delivering blessings to all who love and call upon him.

Meher Baba, "Compassionate Father" demonstrated that love is the great healer. His motto was "mastery through service." Baba traveled throughout India, finding

"God-intoxicants" who were transfixed in spirit, attached to the physical world by the slightest thread. Such people would be considered insane in our culture, but Baba honored their divinity. He washed their feet, fed them, and spoke to their holiness. Meher Baba remained silent for most of life, teaching through the power of his being more than words.

Bruno Gröning demonstrated that anything can be healed, helped countless people miraculously regain their health, and used physical healing as a venue to call people back to their spiritual path. He accepted no money and gave all credit to God. Even after his physical death, many continue to be healed as they access the power he released. Gröning's teaching is refreshingly simple, humble, pure, and free of intellectual gymnastics. While he endured many personal hardships, he maintained a joyful, faithful, positive attitude.

Paramahansa Yogananda courageously left his native India to deliver the message and techniques of yoga to the western world. While some scorned the yogi, many people embraced the skills and transformed their lives. Yogananda was a masterful, well-disciplined, high-integrity teacher who rose above worldly challenges to remain true to his faith. He was ecumenical, honoring all paths to the mountaintop of truth. His book *Autobiography of a Yogi* stands as a metaphysical classic. The organization he established, Self-Realization Fellowship, endures to this day, purely sharing the message of yoga with those who wish to receive it.

My mentor **Hilda Charlton** was continuously available to all who sought her healing. She wanted nothing more than to help others become free. Like Bruno Gröning, she never accepted any money for her services. Her unique spiritual path was self-styled as she trusted her inner guidance more than any external authority. Her sense of humor delighted her students, "the sugar coating on the pill" of spiritual teaching. Hilda allowed the people in greatest pain to be close to her, and worked with them intensively. She maintained a lofty spiritual awareness even while teaching in a crime-ridden area of New York. Hilda lived with her head in the clouds and her feet on the ground, remembering God while dealing masterfully with mundane matters.

Pure healers do walk the earth. If you know one, accept the grace they offer. If you do not know one personally, accept the blessings of one you believe in. Healing does not depend on physical proximity. There is no time or space in spirit. Every great healer who has ever lived is available to you now, their gifts offered to you freely. Such spiritual masters do not seek our worship, but want us to know our *worthship*. They do not inculcate followers, but leaders. They are wayshowers who provide us with models to emulate so we may access the same healing power from which they drew their strength, and pass it along to a waiting world.

Healing Beyond Numbers

Healed healers are more concerned with the quality of their service than the number of their clients. The volume of recipients is not the purpose of a service; it is a byproduct. I never intend or pray for a particular number of participants in my programs. I pray for the right people, those who can most benefit and contribute to the group's purpose. Sometimes that number is high and sometimes it is lower. I value authenticity, connection, building relationships, and healing. This is not to say that you cannot achieve these values in a large group; you just have to stay highly focused and be dedicated to service above all else. If you get the numbers but lose your peace, you cannot call yourself successful. If you keep your head on straight and your heart open no matter how many people show up, you win the grand prize. When you are committed to healing above all, you will be supported in miraculous ways. You will sleep well at night, knowing you are right with yourself and the universe.

Hail to the Chief

While many people believe that the first words that came to channel Helen Schucman were "This is a course in miracles," the introductory phrase she actually received was even more poignant and personal: "I will work miracles through your hands." This statement identifies "I" as God doing the work, and "your hands" as the human conduit through which God delivers healing. God calls us to facilitate transformation, which makes our role crucial.

A Course in Miracles Lesson 353 asks us to affirm, "My eyes, my tongue, my hands, my feet today have but one purpose; to be given Christ to use to bless the world with miracles." This uplevels our body to become an instrument of the divine. Some religious factions attack the body as evil and attempt to beat it into submission through psychological or physical self-flagellation. But the body is neutral; it is what we use it for that determines its good or evil. The body's highest function is that of a venue of communication to express the divine in the world. As long as we walk in bodies, we must make the best use of them. Then God will work miracles through our hands.

You have already delivered miracles to the world. You have spoken words and performed acts of compassion and kindness that brought your fellow human beings relief, diminished their fear, and encouraged them to carry on in the face of adversity, and triumph over it. The ego would have you believe that you are worthless, damaged, or inadequate. It maintains its petty kingdom by keeping you focused on what's wrong with you and what's not working. Yes, you have your quirks and issues, and you have made errors like all of us. But there is far more in you that is functioning perfectly than is not. You are supremely important to God's plan. To realize the magnitude of your mission turns the tide of guilt and suffering in your life, and blesses those you touch.

Don't Wait

Many people hesitate to offer healing because they are not perfect; they are waiting to become qualified. Yet even while you are moving through your own process, you can help the world. I coach many people who are inspired to offer services in alternative medicine, energy work, coaching, teaching, public speaking, seminar leading, mentoring, entrepreneurship, leadership, writing, or artistic expression. Yet they feel unworthy because they have not yet fully mastered their discipline. I tell them that it is not hypocritical to teach a skill you have not yet completely developed as long as you are honest about where you stand on the continuum of learning. Just teach what you know. You will help more people that way than if you wait until you stand at the vanguard of your profession. One of the ways to get to that vanguard is to teach, for in teaching we learn. Albert Einstein felt stymied by some advanced physics problems, but he did not withhold what he had learned to that point. A child sent Einstein a letter complaining that he was having a hard time in his math class. Einstein wrote back, "Do not worry about your difficulties in mathematics. I can assure you mine are still greater."

When you show up to teach or heal, the universe will arrange the details. Your clients or students will find you. The adage, "When the student is ready, the teacher appears" is absolutely true. Likewise, when the teacher is ready, the students appear. The Law of Attraction will join you with those to whom you can be of greatest service, and from whom you can benefit. Healer/client relationships are not random. They are masterfully organized by an intelligence greater than you and I can fathom. If God gave you gifts to share, the people they are meant for will find you. There is no slippage in this impeccably orchestrated system.

Self-care Equals Client Care

Many healers sacrifice their well-being for the sake of their clients. When this happens, ego has hijacked your sacred mission. A burnt-out healer is an oxymoron. Mature healers recognize the importance of self-renewal, and practice it. If you were raised in a family or religion that glorified self-sacrifice, you may believe that for others to win, you must lose. Nothing could be further from the truth. Either we all win together or no one wins.

To be an uplifter, you must be uplifted. Abraham teaches that you cannot get sick enough to make someone else well; miserable enough to make someone else happy; poor enough to make someone else rich; dead enough to make someone else live. Those are all old, outmoded paradigms we must grow beyond to enter the kingdom. You stimulate the health of others by your own health; their joy by yours; their wealth by your model of abundance. When you show your clients or patients how good it can get, they will be inspired to manifest their own good. The best compliment you can receive as a healer or teacher is, "You are shining and thriving. How can I get what you have?"

Self-care is not a sin; self-abuse is. Setting healthy boundaries, resting, taking vacations, getting together with people you love, and enjoying massages, healing treatments, and other self-nurturing activities are all huge contributions to helping others heal. When we model wellness, we teach well.

Where True Joy Lives

One of the greatest rewards of a lifetime is to participate in relieving the suffering of other human beings and help them find greater joy. When you become a vessel for God to do the great work, your own problems disappear. The self-involved "I" dissolves and love fills the space it vacates.

One of the happiest people I have ever seen is Duska, a German woman who runs an orphanage in the poor town of Urubamba, Peru. Adventurer Leon Logothetis introduces Duska in his Netflix series, *The Kindness Diaries* (Season 3, Episode 8). As Duska cares for children without parents, her face shines like a saint. If ever there is proof that giving healing heals the healer, Duska is it.

Many of my life coach trainees report a similar experience. After a few months of practice coaching sessions, many report, "I now know what I was born to do. I am finding the greatest reward of my life." Humanitarian Albert Schweitzer said, "The only ones among you who will be really happy are those who will have sought and found how to serve."

The world is insane and seems to be getting crazier. The contrast between light and dark, illusion and truth, fear and love, is becoming sharper and starker. For that reason, anyone who delivers any healing or upliftment founded in higher values is essential to planetary transformation. Your role is crucial in the great awakening. Now is the time to give your gifts generously and unapologetically.

Healed healers do exist. You can find one and you can be one. Search not for a healer, but for healing. Be not a seeker of persons, but of truth. As you let yourself be healed, you will heal. This is why you came to the world. In the end, all events and experiences reveal themselves to be in the service of this golden quest.

MASTER KEYS *of* THIS CHAPTER

1. Divinely appointed healers with integrity walk this world. When you find one, you are blessed.

2. The list of traits of healed healers noted at the beginning of this chapter is extremely important. Meditate on these attributes to discern between wounded healers and healed healers, and maximize your own healing service.

3. The healer's quality of teaching is not determined by a number of followers, but by the positive life change the healer generates in those he or she touches, be they few or many.

4. Great Spirit can and will work healing and miracles through you. The purpose of your life is to serve as a vehicle through which God can bless the world.

5. Don't wait to step into your healing service. Higher Power will support you and the Law of Attraction will bring the right people to you.

6. Self-care is an essential element in a healed healer's life. A burnt-out healer is an oxymoron. You heal most effectively by your being and your model of wellness.

7. There is no competition in healing. A healer does not have to be right by making other healers wrong. Healed healers are team players and want only the patient's healing.

8. The happiest people in the world are those who make other's lives easier.

SOUL DOCTORS

How far that little candle throws his beams!
So shines a good deed in a weary world.

—WILLIAM SHAKESPEARE

My friend Mark is a physician who was vacationing on Maui when he received a phone call that his nephew, in Honolulu on his own vacation with his wife, had a heart attack and was in the intensive care unit, near death. Hearing this, Mark flew to Honolulu and sat with his nephew's distraught wife at his bedside for 24 hours until her husband stabilized.

As Mark recounted this story, I recognized the distinction between a doctor and a healer. A doctor treats the body. A healer treats the soul. Mark's commitment to the well-being of his nephew and his wife went far beyond fixing the man's body. His gift was to soothe their souls.

A Course in Miracles defines healing as release from fear. Whenever you help someone increase love and decrease fear, you are facilitating healing. If your client remains in fear, or your interaction increases their fear, you are adding not to their healing, but to their illness. You cannot choose for your client, but you can hold a sacred space that maximizes her potential to choose healing.

A healer is a soother. Anything you do that helps your client relax into well-being is healing. One day my dog

Munchie wandered into the territory of a big mean dog, who bit Munchie and ripped a large chunk of his skin off his side. I rushed Munchie to a local veterinarian, whom I'll call Dr. Brown, a nice fellow but a worrier. Dr. Brown operated on Munchie, sewed up his side, and sent him home. A few days later pus began to ooze from the stitched area, indicating it had become infected; the skin that had been reattached was slipping away. I took the dog back to Dr. Brown, who went into a lecture about how there had been a recent upsurge of fecal bacteria in the area, which increased the chance of infection. He operated again and sent Munchie home with antibiotics. A few days later, to my dismay, the symptoms reappeared. I brought my dog back to Dr. Brown for a third surgery. Again the symptoms recurred.

At that point I realized that the dog was not getting better under this veterinarian's care. I could not imagine putting Munchie through any more surgeries—there had to be a better way. I knew of another veterinarian down the road, whom I'll call Dr. Green, a lifelong horse doctor who extended his practice to other pets. I took Munchie to Dr. Green's office, placed him on the examining table, and nervously awaited the doctor. Finally he entered. An older, seasoned cowboy with leathery skin, clad in jeans and a flannel shirt with a small belly hanging over his belt, Dr. Green had a kindly twinkle in his eye, the grandfather we all wished for. He looked at Munchie's wound, turned to me, and read my anxiety. He smiled and softly asked, "Isn't nature wonderful?"

Stunned by his comment, I looked at him with an unspoken question.

He smiled again. "Your dog's gonna be alright."

I can hardly describe the relief that washed over my soul. "He doesn't need any more surgeries?"

The vet shook his head. "No. You can let the wound stay open. I'll give you some pennyroyal to put on the area a few times a day. Keep him in the house, keep him clean, and you'll see over a week or two the skin will grow back over the wound."

I wanted to kiss the man. Maybe I did. I took Munchie in my arms and brought him home. Sure enough, as I followed Dr. Green's instructions, over the following week the skin gradually grew back over the wound and sewed itself up perfectly. No more surgeries. No infections. Just healing. A few years later I dedicated one of my books, subtitled *What I Learned from the World's Richest Man,* to Dr. Green. The title is, *How Good Can It Get?*

I learned valuable lessons from this harrowing but enlightening experience. One was to work with a doctor you believe in, who is more dedicated to healing than illness. Another was the powerful relationship between intention and results. It was only when I was totally frustrated and fed up with not getting results that my intention became so strong that I was willing to do whatever I needed to achieve wellness, including changing doctors if necessary. A third lesson was that sometimes natural, old-fashioned, organic remedies work where medical technologies do not. The final lesson, which has stayed with me at a core level, is that a healer is a soother. A true healer touches not just the client's body, but his soul. In the case of Munchie, Dr. Green spoke directly to my soul and that of my beloved companion.

Where Healing Meets Doctoring

Being a soul doctor does not preclude being a physical doctor. You can be both. The question is one of priorities. Is it more important to fix the body, or the soul? Obviously it is important to address both. But fixing only the body is temporary. If you do not address the soul, symptoms will reappear or pop up elsewhere. When the soul is healed, the body generally follows.

Psalm 23 asks us to remember, "He restores my soul." While this affirmation may sound simply like biblical poetry, it is one of the most practical, grounded, earthy healing tools you will ever receive. We become sick when our soul is left unattended; the pain and burdens of our life outweigh the joys. While many people exhibit physical and psychological symptoms of illness, behind them is sickness of the soul. Your soul cannot really be sick, for it is an expression of a perfect God. But you can become so disconnected from your soul that you lose touch with the life force it offers you.

When people attend one of my programs, especially the in-person residential retreats, many get their soul back. They relax, release their burdens, connect with like-minded peers, express their passion, play, edify their spiritual path, immerse themselves in nature, and come alive. I have seen many people lose 10 or 20 years from their face in the course of a week. Struggling ages, and relaxation youthens. You don't have to attend one of my programs to get your soul back. You can restore your life force anytime you quit stressing and start loving and caring for yourself. And if you help another human being get their soul back, whether you are a doctor or a store clerk, you are a healer.

The Circle of Healing

My friend Don is a radio personality who has hosted his popular music show in a large city for many years. In addition to playing hit songs, he daily reads an inspirational message on the air. He is well known and loved in his community.

Recently Don went through a severe bout with depression. One day he revealed to his radio listeners that he was depressed and having a tough time. The next day Don received an email from the director of a psychiatric hospital. She told Don, "Thank you for courageously sharing about your emotional challenge. I know this can be a very difficult process to go through. I am certain that you helped many of your listeners who are dealing with the same experience, giving them permission to authentically express their feelings, which is the first step to healing. I have enjoyed your show for many years, especially the inspirational quotes you share. I hope you will continue to progress and feel better."

Don was deeply touched by this email, as I was when he shared it with me. This psychiatrist, obviously busy in a position of high importance, did not have to take the time and care to send Don such a supportive note. But she did. I told Don, "This woman is a real healer."

This healing process was built on a dynamic cycle that began with Don sharing his difficulty with his radio audience—an act of courage and vulnerability. Many radio show hosts succumb to silly banter and shallow stories peppered with phony laughter. Don's sincere expression got his audience's attention, typified by the psychiatrist who wrote to him as a spokesperson for the positive effect he had on his audience. The blessing came full circle when the doctor gifted Don with support and encouragement.

Heal Where You Stand

You don't need to be a professional healer to be a soul doctor. You can soothe souls right where you stand. *A Course in Miracles* tells us that when you perform a miracle—meaning

that you choose love over fear and create a positive result—
"it may touch many people you have not even met, and
produce undreamed of changes in situations of which
you are not even aware." You can heal as a school crossing
guard, realtor, or taxi driver. One of my coach graduates is
a divorce attorney who uses her coaching skills to help her
clients keep their marriage together or, if they are intent on
divorcing, guide them to do so with harmony, respect, and
mutual support. Another graduate integrates holistic coaching with financial planning. Some YouTube videos chronicle
extraordinary acts of kindness, like the Thai policeman who
responded to a distraught knife attacker by gently asking for
the knife, getting him a glass of water, hugging him, giving
him a guitar, and taking him to dinner. ("Thai Police Offi-
cer Disarms Man with Knife with a Hug") Another inspiring
video shows a jeweler who was approached by a frazzled
mother seeking to sell an heirloom ring because she had no
money to support her family. The jeweler reached into his
pocket, took out a wad of cash, gave it to the woman, and
told her to keep the ring. ("Syrian Muslim Man Pays for U.S.
Woman Desperate to Sell her Ring in Dallas")

Every day we all have many opportunities to offer healing. You don't need to prescribe a drug or lay on hands. You
just need to recognize that the people you meet are souls
more than they are bodies, and offer kindness to the part of
them that needs it most.

More than a Machine

Doctors who overlook the souls of their patients overlook their own souls. Doctors who remember their patients'
souls save their own. Western medicine loses its soul when it
treats people like machines only. The body is a machine, but

there is someone who lives in the body, a being precious far beyond the sum of the body's part. Every human being is an expression of the vast intelligence that put the body together and maintains it. Doctors who lose touch with their soul become miserable; you can't restrict your vision to bodies all day every day and retain your awareness of spirit. Sadly, the rate of drug abuse among doctors is among the highest in the professions. Doctors have many pressures on them. If they don't have tools to rise beyond those pressures, they may exhibit tragic results. When they learn healthy ways to address their stress, they regain their souls and help their patients regain theirs.

While some people regard the soul as some mysterious, etheric, nebulous, other-world entity, its reality is obvious even as we walk the earth. It is the very essence of who we all are. When you look into your child's eyes for the first time, you see far more than a little body. When a gifted performer sings, dances, acts, writes, speaks, or paints from their core, you feel something far richer than when a performer simply goes through the motions. At a fundamental level we all know what the soul is because it is the core of our being. The more we treat each other as souls rather than bodies, the more meaning we find in our life. If you truly wish to be healed, do what gives your life meaning. The physical world is hollow until we recognize the spiritual opportunities it offers us. Then it comes alive with wonder and possibility. When you remember your soul, you know why you are here, and when you touch another person's soul, you remind them why they are here. Nothing less will bring us the fulfillment we seek.

MASTER KEYS *of* THIS CHAPTER

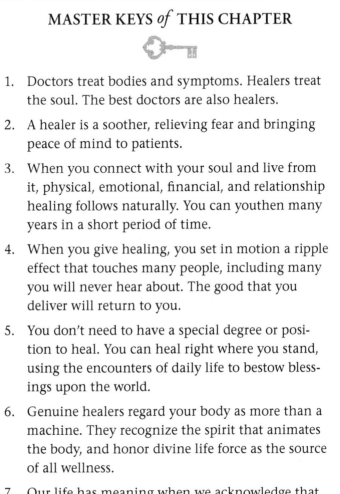

1. Doctors treat bodies and symptoms. Healers treat the soul. The best doctors are also healers.

2. A healer is a soother, relieving fear and bringing peace of mind to patients.

3. When you connect with your soul and live from it, physical, emotional, financial, and relationship healing follows naturally. You can youthen many years in a short period of time.

4. When you give healing, you set in motion a ripple effect that touches many people, including many you will never hear about. The good that you deliver will return to you.

5. You don't need to have a special degree or position to heal. You can heal right where you stand, using the encounters of daily life to bestow blessings upon the world.

6. Genuine healers regard your body as more than a machine. They recognize the spirit that animates the body, and honor divine life force as the source of all wellness.

7. Our life has meaning when we acknowledge that we are souls more than bodies.

THE CHOICE FOR COMPLETION

*The whole truth is this: the time
of the half-life is over. Done.
There's no more time for half-hearted living, half-truths
and dividing life into neat compartments. We have work to
do here. It begins from the inside-out, with a commitment
to see ourselves as whole and to embrace the fullness of
who we are and who we are becoming.*

—DAWN RICHERSON

The colorful documentary *Unbranded* unfurls the saga
of four young Texans who set out to ride horses bor-
der-to-border from Mexico to Canada. For months these
bold adventurers prepared for their rigorous journey, training wild mustangs, gathering provisions, and mapping their
3,000-mile epic threading through many western states.
Finally the momentous spring day came and they set out
into the unknown, hardships and triumphs before them.
The cowboys roamed through vast stunning spaces; lived,
ate, and slept in the cradle of nature; and bonded with
each other and their steeds. They endured harsh weather,
daunting climbs up rugged mountains, interpersonal conflicts, and the callousness of a rancher who would not let
them pass through his property, forcing them to plod a

grueling roundabout route for days. At one point one of the horses died.

Finally, after a demanding four-month trek, the troupe approached the Canadian border, where their families had gathered to greet and congratulate them. Just a mile from the border, one of the riders did something quite bizarre: he stopped. He refused to complete the trip. When his buddies asked him why, he answered, "It's better to leave something for next time." His stopping and statement made no sense whatsoever. His rationale was a thin veil for the fear of completion.

Some of us are so enamored with going somewhere that we would not know what to do if we got there. The ego, founded in the belief in lack, demands a gap to maintain its identity. The spirit, by contrast, thrives on a sense of wholeness. The ego cites a goal it has not yet reached. The spirit claims that the goal is not just reachable, but reached. The ego swears, "One day I will be there." The spirit declares, "I am there."

Disease is a form of incompletion. "Part of me is broken and needs fixing or replacement. If this organ worked better, I would feel good and my life would work." Of course, it is so. Yet how you define yourself in your healing process constitutes a huge element of your progress. One of your organs may be malfunctioning at the moment. But there is a you that is greater, stronger, and freer than that organ. You are not limited by what's happening in your physical body. Even while your body goes through its experience, you dwell in a spiritual reality that cannot be ill, flawed, empty, or broken. The real you never was and never will be sick. Your eternal spirit is impervious to the conditions that physical existence shouts. The real you is all that God is. No other attribute does justice to the masterpiece that God created.

You are either whole or you are not. That is what healing comes down to. Certainly we have our human journey. We strive for good health, a secure home, financial success, career fulfillment, a loving partnership and family, and the many good things that life has to offer. Those endeavors will not stop. There will always be something else to reach for. Yet, as you have probably noticed, reaching never ends. I interviewed Dominic Miller, the guitarist in Sting's band. For years Dominic trotted the globe with the celebrated group in a private jet with lavish amenities. "No matter how good it got, I was always thinking 'there must be more,'" Dominic recounted. "As our band was cruising in a sleek Learjet 60, our conversation became, 'Wouldn't it really be cool if we could get a 70?'" No matter how good it gets, the ego chides that you could do better. While striving is natural and healthy, our *attitude behind the striving* determines whether the journey is one of angst or reward. If you can maintain a sense of appreciation and celebration while you reach for your goal, you have it made. If you are waiting for the next thing to complete you, you will remain unfulfilled. While we don't always have a choice about our circumstances, we always have a choice about how we view our circumstances. D.H. Lawrence aptly stated,

> Those that go searching for love
> only make manifest their own lovelessness,
> and the loveless never find love,
> only the loving find love,
> and they never have to seek for it.

We might say the same of health: Those who seek health tend to continue to seek it, while those who find health continue to find it. This is not to suggest that if you feel ill you should not seek health. To the contrary, this dynamic contains the key to find it. You will have more success coming *from* health than heading *toward* it. A famous basketball player was asked, "How do you score so many points?" He answered, "The ball is in the basket before it leaves my hand." When you *see* the healthy you, you will *be* the healthy you.

Beyond the Fear of Completion

Because the ego is built on the belief in a space between where you are and where you want to be, its greatest fear is completion. So it avoids, denies, and sabotages finishing. This is one of the causes of procrastination or not striving for your valued goal. It seems more comfortable to leave things undone. But in the long run not finishing saps life force. I once noticed a ceiling light fixture in my house that needed repair. I purchased a replacement, which sat in a closet for a long time. Every time I looked at the light fixture, I thought, "I need to get to that." When I finally did, the project took just 20 minutes. Looking back, I realized that all the times I thought, "I need to get to that" added up to way, way more than 20 minutes, not to mention the niggling empty feeling that there was something I needed to achieve before I could really enjoy my home. Leaving things undone often costs us more than doing them.

Lest you believe that you must finish all of your projects now, and become a slave to your to-do list, remember that completion is more a state of mind than an act. You can choose to feel complete even before you finish your endless list of tasks. My computer repairman's workspace appears to be a huge mess. Gerry has countless keyboards, hard drives, cables, and dead computers stacked almost from floor to ceiling in his crowded man cave. When I visit him, I have to wend my way through a waist-high maze of machines to get to his desk. Yet, amazingly, when he needs a part, he knows exactly where to find it; he just steps to a pile in the corner and pulls it from the bottom like a file neatly labeled in a tidy file cabinet. Gerry is at peace with himself, his methodology, and his cluttered space. Meanwhile he is brilliant and efficient. Whenever I need a hardware or software fix, he nails it. In his own way, Gerry lives in the experience of completion even while, from an observer's view, he seems far from it.

Your affairs can be in perfect order, but if you feel hollow, anxious, or waiting, you are incomplete. On the other hand, your affairs can seem to be disordered, but if you are established in a sense of enoughness, you are working efficiently and peacefully. We cannot judge by appearances. What your body is doing is far less important than what your mind is doing. Here is a powerful affirmation I like and use:

There is nothing I need to do first to become complete.
I am whole, perfect, and at peace with myself
and my life right now.

At the Mountaintop

You will not achieve wholeness by doing more. You will achieve wholeness by knowing you *are* more. This is why spiritual masters call enlightenment "self-realization" or "self-actualization." The journey of life culminates in coming home to your true self. *A Course in Miracles* tells us if you drop into your inherent enoughness even for a few moments, you can save a thousand years of striving. Wow, take a moment to take that in! You can avoid lifetimes of karma by recognizing that the perfection you seek already lives within you, as you. This is the short route to enlightenment—steep in that it asks you to move vertically rather than horizontally—but radically effective in that you quit circling the base of the mountain, and rise to the peak.

Even the thought that there is a mountain to climb is an illusion. There is no mountain. You already stand at the summit. The ego made up a story that there is somewhere to get, and you went about the strenuous, even humorous journey of trying to reach where you already are. The ego fears completion because it equates completion with death. To ensure its survival, it keeps finding projects to avoid death. Sarah Winchester, widow of firearm magnate William Wirt Winchester, believed that if she did not keep building rooms onto her house, she would die. So the wealthy heiress kept adding rooms 24/7, sprinting feverishly to avoid the grim reaper. To this day you can visit her sprawling mansion in San Jose, California. Rumors have it that the place is haunted by the ghosts of all the people killed by Winchester rifles. More metaphysically, it is haunted by all of Sarah Winchester's fears of death by completion. Ghostly thoughts pose a far greater danger than ectoplasmic spooks. If you want to do some serious ghostbusting, bust your thoughts of not-enoughness.

Like Sarah Winchester, a part of our mind believes that if we accepted completion, we would die. But the truth is, if we accepted completion, we would live. We would live *from* wholeness instead of running after it. In a sense, if we accepted completion, we would die, in that we would lose interest in a world built on striving for what we already have, in places we will never find it. We would die to the world of appearances, which crucifies us, and be resurrected in the world of wholeness, which restores us. We would no longer care about reaching out because we would be so satisfied reaching in. The world of struggle would lose its grip on us and we would cease to be fixated on emptiness. The ego is correct in equating completion with death—not the death of the body, but the death of fear.

Jesus said, "Even greater things than I, shall you do," indicating that when we recognize our enoughness as clearly as he recognized his, the same Power that moved through him will move through us. Jesus and other great masters could heal others because they saw no gap between who they were and who they could be. Those healers saw their patients as whole, so they became whole. If you wish to heal yourself or others, become whole by knowing you *are* whole. In the big picture, nothing is missing. You are not just close to the border. You are across it. Don't stop to leave something for next time. There is no next time. Healing is now.

MASTER KEYS *of* THIS CHAPTER

1. The ego creates a false sense of incompletion that makes it seem as if there is a gap between where you stand and where you want to be. Because that gap is a lie, it will never be crossed. You cannot fix what is already whole.

2. Even while you go through your human journey of seeking, striving, and reaching higher, you are already complete.

3. Disease is a form of incompletion, as it denies our inherent wholeness.

4. The more you seek health, the more it eludes you. The more you claim health, the more you experience it.

5. Completion is more of a state of mind than a condition. It is possible to live in a state of divine sufficiency even while you go through your worldly activities of getting things done.

6. Enlightenment recognizes that you already stand at the mountaintop you thought you had to strive to reach.

DEATH AND HEALING

*Of one thing I am certain, the body is not
the measure of healing, peace is the measure.*

—PHYLLIS MCGINLEY

When I studied with gifted healer Alberto Aguas, he mentioned that two of his most powerful healings occurred with people who passed on soon afterward. A student asked, "If these people died, how can you say they were healed?" Alberto answered, "They came to deep inner peace. Their bodies fell away, but their spirits were soaring." A well body is desirable, but a well mind is crucial. If your soul is at peace, no matter what your body is doing, you have found the pearl of great price.

I have never been a big fan of death; I have avoided it where I can. Then Dee and I moved to a very rural area where we were clearly the minority: there were two of us, and millions of animals surrounding us: horses, cattle, pigs, goats, sheep, feral cats, geckos, all kinds of birds, and an endless array of crawly bugs. Immediately we became very aware that lots of these critters were dying daily, from predation and natural causes. Native Hawaiians were hunting on the property next to ours. Then I looked out on the vast ocean and realized that at every moment trillions of living things were eating and being eaten by others. Death was inescapable.

This encounter moved me to confront death in ways I never had. I wondered, "In a world with so much death, what is life?" One of my coach trainees succinctly answered this question for me with a grisly but illuminating account. He reported, "In the army I was assigned to a team that rushed to the sites of experimental airplanes that had crashed. My job was to clean up the human remains. The job was grim, but I came to a stunning realization: The body parts I was picking up were not the person who lived in them. A spiritual being greater than flesh and bone had animated them. There had to be more to life than perishable organs. With that insight, a huge peace coursed through me and I took a major step ahead on my own spiritual journey."

I had a similar—and far gentler—awakening. My friend Raymond was a tall, strapping, good-looking fellow in his late twenties. He oozed vitality and I always felt uplifted in his presence. One day I learned that Raymond had died suddenly of a rare disease he had been dealing with for years. I was stunned; just a few days ago I was laughing, eating, and sharing stories with my friend. Then he was gone in a flash. I had a hard time making sense of this shocking turn of events.

As I pondered this dilemma, I realized that Raymond could not be alive and then dead. His body, yes; but there was so much more to him than his body. I reasoned that either Raymond was always here or he was never here. His life force was too real to deny. His energetic presence was not caused by his body; his body was the vehicle through which his presence flowed. I came to the conclusion that Raymond's life was real but his death was not. This makes no sense in a reality defined by the physical senses only—when you're dead, you're dead. But from a higher perspective, when you're alive, you're always alive.

There is far more to healing than you and I have been told. Life is more metaphysical than physical—we live from the inside out, from mind to feeling to physical experience. To attempt to heal at the physical level only is severely short-sighted. Real healing penetrates to our core.

Death as a Choice

One of the frightening aspects of death is that we believe it is cast upon us by a dark foreign will greater than our own. Yet spiritual teachers tell us that we choose the duration of our life and the moment of our death. This does not appear to be so, as we observe people killed by diseases, wars, crimes, and accidents. Yet the surface level of life is but an expression of choices we make at a soul level, which the eye cannot see and the intellect cannot fathom. When a student asked Abraham about a friend who had committed suicide, Abraham explained, "All death is suicide," meaning that every person who dies is at choice about the event, rather than a victim of an external agent. The overt act of suicide is just a dramatic expression of a choice to depart that we all make. Some people drink themselves to death or trigger drug overdoses; others impair their decision-making ability and end up in car crashes; others generate stress-related diseases; and others just fade away.

My friends had a dog who lived to the phenomenal age of 22. Then the dog's systems broke down to the point that the veterinarian recommended euthanasia. My friends were reluctant to have the dog put down, and avoided the event until they could put it off no longer. They lovingly placed their frail companion in the back seat of their car and drove to the vet's office for the dreaded task. When they parked the car, they opened the rear door to find that the dog had expired. It let them know that it was ready, and spared them the pain and possible guilt of putting the dog down.

This is not to say that you should not put a pet down. In some cases this is the kindest act. I cite the above story to illustrate that we, as well as our furry companions, have more choice about our departure than we have been led to believe. Some people hang in there until they know their loved ones are well taken care of, or their son gets married, or the grandbaby comes. Others have lost their passion and give way to an apparently life-threatening disease. Then they fall in love, or have a spiritual awakening, or feel the power of their loved ones' prayers, or experience some other jolt of life force. Suddenly they are in the game again; doctors are amazed at how the disease disappeared. Wellness, disease, and death are far more choices than we have been told.

A Graceful Exit

My neighbor Tom recently passed away at the age of 88. He lay down to take a nap one afternoon, and he didn't wake up—a truly graceful exit. Tom was fully alive and extremely active until that moment. He held the distinction of being the oldest volunteer firefighter in the state. When his peers urged him to retire, he answered, "I'll retire when I'm ready to, and not a day before." Tom demonstrated a model I have heard Abraham suggest: "Happy, healthy, happy, healthy, happy, healthy . . . dead."

Tom's gentle passage represents an exception to the way that most people depart. Most die at the end of a lingering illness or in a dramatic moment. Let's rethink why this is so. I have suggested that we must question, challenge, and grow beyond the limiting beliefs we have been taught about health and illness. Likewise, we must question and grow beyond the limiting ideas we have been shown about how to die. We have been taught by model that we exit by way of pain, struggle, and drama. But what if those elements are not required? What if they represent beliefs more than realities? What if we could depart as quietly and painlessly as Tom? Imagine that you can leave this world in a gentle way that you choose, rather than a painful way chosen for you. How freeing is that vision?

There are other variables that could affect your method and timing of departure. The wishes and attachments of loved ones may influence your exit strategy. A student of Abraham asked Esther Hicks, channel for Abraham, why Esther's husband Jerry took a year to depart through a long illness. Abraham explained that Jerry was giving Esther time to adjust to his passing; if the event had occurred suddenly, it might have been overwhelming to her.

Others decide it's time to go, no matter what's going on around them. One of my teachers told me, "I'm old. I'm tired. I want to go home." Within a year he was gone.

The idea of "going home" is the most apt and comforting metaphor to reframe death. The Earth is not our home. We are spiritual beings temporarily visiting this planet. While the world offers many beauties and wonders, it also yields pain and sorrow. Buddha's first noble truth is that life involves suffering. I have heard, "Everyone is hurting somehow; some people are just better at pretending." While we might wish for physical immortality, ultimately it would be unattractive, since the world as we know it is largely a denial of spirit, and when we deny spirit, we suffer. Would you really want to live in a body forever? Or would you at some point prefer to throw off the mortal coil and return to pure positive energy?

Eventually everyone chooses to go home to God. We call it death. Others call it "the great return." My mentor used to say, "When a baby is born, people rejoice and the angels cry. When someone dies, people cry and the angels rejoice." The world, *A Course in Miracles* tells us, is the inverse of heaven; what seems real and solid here is insubstantial and meaningless in heaven. "Not one thing the world believes is true," the Course states. While the world tells us that the body is our home, higher wisdom tells us that the spirit is our home. While immersion in body consciousness is the rule of the world, it is only when we become immersed in spirit consciousness that we are fulfilled.

The Soul has its Reasons

The great return sounds comforting when we consider people who live long and fulfilling lives. They are done with their earthly journey, their body no longer serves them, and they are ready to move on. But what about children who die at a young age? Didn't they have the right to live out a long and fulfilling life?

In such cases, the child may have just had a little business to do on Earth. One of my mentors said that such a soul "just wanted to dip his foot into the waters of life for a moment." From a human standpoint this makes no sense; we are deeply saddened when a child comes and goes quickly. Yet in the grand scope of eternity, is a year really that much less time than 80? Through human eyes, certainly. From a broader perspective, we are all eternal beings. Our life in God far transcends our life on Earth, be that a short or long term in human counting. We cannot know the purpose of a soul's journey; that is between that soul and God. The intellect, designed to navigate and survive the physical world, hits an impassable wall when it attempts to understand matters of the spirit, which requires a far deeper mind to fathom. You will not find mental answers to spiritual questions. The soul has its own reasons.

Dealing with death forces us to face and answer deeper questions. It moves us to think about what is really important. People who have experienced the death of a loved one, or face their own death, usually deepen in compassion, appreciate life more, and value their relationships. A Buddhist monk suggested, "Contemplate your death to enhance the quality of your life."

Love Never Dies

Our relationships with loved ones do not end with the cessation of their physical body, or ours. The relationship simply moves to a higher octave. You become closer to the other person because you are no longer limited to where your bodies are located. Your loved ones are very much with you; they have not gone very far, just on the other side of a curtain. In some of my seminars I ask the audience, "Who among you has received some communication from a loved one after they passed on?" Most of the people in the audience raise their hands. When we remain connected with a dear one after they have departed the physical world, the spiritual reality demonstrates itself as real.

The physical world is the tiniest slice of creation, a dream that dissolves the moment we awaken. The body will age and die. So what? Your spirit was never born, cannot age, and will never die. Death is real to the body, but not to the soul that animates it. The reality and immortality of the soul are the doors to healing. If you believe you are a body only, you will seek to heal the body at the level of the body, and try to get rid of symptoms by physical means such as pills and various manipulations, which certainly help. Yet to be permanently healed we must work from the inside out. When you tap into your spiritual essence, you have infinitely more leverage to heal than you do when you work at the physical level only.

Many years after viewing that pile of chemical remains in my college library, I wonder if the man whose body they once formed ever discovered that he was more than his heartbeat and sexual experiences. Did his human journey lead to a greater identity than he associated with his body? Did he ever glimpse the vaster panorama of existence? I will never know how far he came on his path of self-knowledge. And he will never know the gift that his remains imparted to me, and now, perhaps, to you. Or perhaps he does.

MASTER KEYS *of* THIS CHAPTER

1. Death seems real in the world of changing forms. In the reality of spirit, it does not exist.

2. Even though a body may wither and die, if a person's consciousness dwells in inner peace, he or she is healed.

3. A soul is either always alive or it was never alive. It is always alive.

4. The body is an effect, not a cause. Mind is the only cause. Healing is a result of identifying with the mind and spirit, not the body.

5. Death is a choice, never an accident or the result of a fate laid over us by an external source. We choose when we come and we choose when we depart, in co-creation with God.

6. Every soul has its reason and plan for the time and conditions into which it is born, and the time and conditions in which the body is laid aside. A short life, though perplexing and saddening from a human standpoint, fulfills the intention of that soul.

7. It is possible to leave the body gently and gracefully.

8. Because we are souls more than bodies, relationships are forever. Love never dies.

9. It is possible to maintain a relationship with a loved one who has passed on, continue communication, and deepen our connection with them.

HOW TO SAVE
THE WORLD

*Practice kindness all day to everybody and
you will realize you're already in heaven now.*

—JACK KEROUAC

My friend Dennis has walked the fine line between genius and insanity for most of his life. A sensitive, introspective soul, he taps into lofty visions, passionate poetry, and compassion for humanity. At other times his shadow side takes over, he plunges into dark depression, and he holes up in his apartment for months at a time.

One day I received a phone call from Dennis telling me he had been locked up in a mental hospital, and he wanted me to visit him. I drove to the facility and we had some quiet time together. "What happened that got you locked up?" I asked him.

"I felt quite disoriented and came to the emergency room," he replied.

"But you've done that before," I reminded him. "They gave you meds, released you, and assigned you to a therapist. What was different about this visit?"

Dennis thought for a moment. "Maybe it was how I filled out the intake form."

"What did you say?"

"In the blank where they asked, 'What is your occupation?' I answered, 'world savior.'"

Yep, that would do it.

When someone declares his intention to save the world, he is usually branded crazy, mocked, medicated, or the recipient of an assassin's bullet. Nothing terrifies the world more than someone who wants to heal it; humanity is adamant in its defense of dysfunction. Mahatma Gandhi, one of the most effective world change agents in recent centuries—also cut down by an agent of fear—stated, "We must be the change we wish to see." People who have big ideas about improving life on the planet are usually violently resisted while they live, and sainted after they are gone. The world acknowledges truth only when it cannot bother us in real time. Jesus said, "A prophet is never accepted in his own town." We might also say, "A prophet is never accepted in his own time."

One of *A Course in Miracles'* boldest lessons calls us to remember, "Salvation of the world depends on me." While at first glance this statement may seem arrogant or even delusional, to deny your power to heal is the ultimate arrogance, as it refutes the gifts with which God has entrusted you. Only a humble person would admit that God works through her, for she recognizes that her strength springs from a Source far beyond her small self defined by the physical senses and social labels.

How can one person save the world? The world is so vast, so rife with sorrow and suffering, so complex, so riddled with evil. Surely the influence of one person is paltry in relation to the sea of pain in which humanity writhes. Surely there are many more people out there with more money, power, influence, and guns. It all just seems too overwhelming.

Yet there is one tool in the kit of genuine world saviors that few people recognize: a profound shift in perception.

Authentic healers see beyond appearances and recognize divinity where others see mortality; possibility where others see problems; calls for love where others see attack. You will never save the world by subscribing to the agreements that make the world seem so solid. You must enter into a higher agreement with a vaster Source that refuses to let humanity be damned. To save the world, you must pierce beyond deceptive imagery and recognize the presence of God where others swear it is absent. The choice to see the world through different eyes is the seed of its salvation.

From the Mundane to the Magnificent

One of my most esteemed mentors is the immortal visionary Don Quixote, a soul on fire who rose above the mundane to affirm the magnificent. While the people he encountered mocked him as crazy, he offered them a way of seeing that could help them escape their own insanity. Don Quixote met a harlot named Aldonza, whom he refused to judge as the world did. To him, she was the Lady Dulcinea, "Sweet One." "Don't you know what I am?" the woman scowled as he professed his love to her on bended knee. "Yes, you are my lady, and I am your knight," he declared. Don Quixote's world far transcended social opinions. He saw the woman as he would have her be. The renegade knight chose his domain rather than submitting to the one others would choose for him.

Over time Don Quixote's vision was beaten back by fearful people manipulating him to give up his delusion and join them in theirs. Eventually the twinkle in his eye succumbed to a hollow cavern, his life force waned, and he fell ill, like many who forsake their dreams. When Aldonza came to visit Don Quixote on his deathbed, she was aghast at what had become of this once bold and vital adventurer. Transformed by the purity of his love, now *she* was the vision holder. "Don't you remember the quest?" she asked.

"What quest?" he replied wearily.

"You are Don Quixote, Lord of La Mancha, and I am your Lady Dulcinea."

Hearing those names, a glimmer returned to his sullen eyes and his soul began to stir. The ember on the verge of extinguishing was fanned once more. As Dulcinea continued to remind Don Quixote of his noble vision, his memory awakened and gathered momentum. He leaped out of bed and summoned his sidekick Sancho, "Bring me my armor!"

In a burst of newfound life, Don Quixote, Dulcinea, and Sancho reclaimed their glorious vision. The walls of frailty crumbled and the knight and his love were reunited. Then, as the story would have it, the knight collapsed to his death.

But as observers, we do not feel that his quest has failed. To the contrary, when Don Quixote reclaimed his mission and recognized himself and his love as they truly were, he was the victor. The body perished, but the spirit lived on.

One day all of our bodies will perish, but our spirits will live on. In the meantime, we are called to stay true to our quest while we walk the earth. We are all Don Quixote and Dulcinea, lost in a deluded world, on a sacred journey to reclaim our purpose. As we do, we gain the power to resurrect what once seemed unhealable. Christ and other great visionaries are not exceptions to the destiny of humanity. They are harbingers of the Promised Land we shall all enter. Now they have passed the mantle to us, calling us to mount our steeds, vanquish the dragons that intimidate the fearful, and make a stand for what could be rather than what has been.

You are among the saviors of the world because the realest part of you has never been diminished. Only in the world of illusion has your mission been tattered. Fear cannot thwart the gifts that love came to deliver. *A Course in Miracles* tells us that is it is not what you have been saved *from* that matters, but what you have been saved *for*. The time has come for you to take your armor out of storage and mount your steed. The spiritual warrior's armor is not forged of steel, but integrity. You are protected not by what you made of yourself, but by what you are. The real you has never been tainted. Your soul has remained conscious even while your mind has slept. Now, like Don Quixote, you are regaining your memory. The curtains of amnesia are parting and the sun of truth is piercing the fog of delusion. Your hidden identity is rising to the surface, and you are awakening.

Who Needs to be Healed?

It is tempting to seek to change the world before you change yourself. But upgrading your own consciousness is the key to improving the world. *A Course in Miracles* tells us that the fundamental goal of a miracle worker is the healing of his own mind. If you see a world in need of salvation, your vision is faulty. While to the limited self that world seems quite real and unfixable, that image has no meaning to the Spirit because such a world is fraught with lack, and Spirit is aware only of supply. God's vision soars beyond separation and conflict, the progeny of illusion. The world is the stage upon which the demons of our inner psyche play out their sordid drama; unless those demons are exorcised where they live, they will simply find their way to other stages. To attempt to end external strife before you end internal conflict is as fruitless as charging a screen in a movie theater to end a war movie. Instead, you must address the film from which the images are being projected. You must remove the film from the projector or, better yet, turn on the lights in the theater.

Many people set out to save humanity as a distraction from self-discovery. It seems easier to try to fix others than to confront our own pain and fears. *A Course in Miracles* asks, "Can the world be saved if you are not?" If you want to help someone get out of a hole, you must stand on higher ground to give them a hand. Then you have leverage. If you jump into the hole with them, you both need saving. In a sense, we are all in a hole in that we have forgotten our everlasting connection with God. Until we remember that, we can only shift our location within the hole rather than rise to escape it. We will keep making horizontal moves until we go vertical. Only those connected to their Source are in a position to help.

Already

Saving the world requires mastery of a paradox: The world you seek to save is already saved. The healing you desire has already been accomplished. Well-being is far closer to reality than what you see on the news. To the reasoning mind founded in fear-based thinking, this assertion seems absurd; surely the world has an infinite number of problems that must be resolved before it can be saved. But appearances deny reality as sure as reality denies appearances. Our problem is not logistical; it is perceptual. Twelve-step groups call participants to admit, "I have a [drinking] [drug] [gambling] problem." We can all admit, "I have a perceptual problem." "I see gaps where there is wholeness. I see lack where there is plenty. I see the absence of love where love abides. I see death where there is life." You can't fill gaps in what is already whole. But you can change your vision to acknowledge and celebrate completeness.

What is broken can never be fixed. What is whole can never be broken. You will never make error true, or the physical eternal. Fear and love cannot both be real. You will believe one and deny the other, or deny one and believe the other. *A Course in Miracles* sums up this principle in its introduction:

> Nothing real can be threatened.
>
> Nothing unreal exists.
>
> Herein lies the peace of God.

To save a broken world, you must step into a healed world. To step into a healed world, you must choose healed thoughts. You can spend lifetimes taping Band-Aids on the wounds of humanity, but until you see humanity through the eyes of divinity, there will always be more to fix. When you give up trying to save the world, you will find a peace the world can never deliver. Then you are in the perfect position to save the world because you are aligned with the well-being you wish to establish.

Giving up a lack-based quest for world salvation does not mean you sit around, become a blob, turn a deaf ear to suffering, ignore calls for help, and do nothing. It means that you drop into an inner quietude that gives you access to the guidance to act effectively and serve as many people as possible. True empathy recognizes that there is more to a human being than the part that is suffering. You help at every turn, but do not lose your peace as you go. You may still teach, deliver medical services, sell your product, lecture, write, parent, or do whatever you feel called to do. But instead of proceeding from desperation, you proceed from inspiration. Instead of acting alone, you partner with Higher Power. Instead of trying to change other people so you can feel better, you change your thoughts so you feel better before they change. When you are empowered, you are in the perfect position to empower others.

In the clever movie *Oh, God!* God shows up as a man and asks a befuddled supermarket manager to deliver a message to humanity. God wants Jerry to tell the world that "it can work," meaning that the world can be a peaceful, rewarding, healthy place if we just get our heads out of a dark place and look up. At first Jerry resists, but when he is convinced that God is for real, he agrees. As God is driving Jerry to the site where he will deliver the message, Jerry gets nervous. God places a comforting hand on Jerry's shoulder and tells him, "You have the strength that comes from knowing."

You, too, have the strength that comes from knowing. Even while you may struggle with worldly challenges, a part of you knows what you need to know. Let the knowing part come forth. Even if at first it feels foreign, phony, or forced, if you express your knowing you will see by its manifestations that this element is far more connected to truth than your fearful thoughts. Let God be God in you and through you. When you do, you heal your own life and help others find the well-being they yearn for.

You don't need to be a Jesus, Moses, Mohammed, Albert Schweitzer, or Mother Teresa to deliver the message. You don't even have to believe in God or consider yourself a spiritual person. Some of the most spiritual people I know claim they are atheists, but they are kind and loving and take good care of people and the planet. You just have to quit playing small and claim your identity as a whole, masterful, loving being. All else will follow naturally.

The world will be saved because you are. Not by some miraculous intervention, but by recognizing that miracles happen every day, including through you. When anyone loves, God is showing up in the world. When you open to miracles, they will find you everywhere you turn. You will be healed because as a spiritual being you exist in a state of Grace. You will heal others because you recognize them to be whole, like yourself, far more than bodies, personalities, labels, and erroneous self-images. God is dispatching you into a waiting world and asking you not just to hold up the light, but to *be* the light. Now it's up to you.

MASTER KEYS *of* THIS CHAPTER

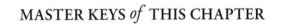

1. World healing proceeds from the inside out. While it appears that we must save the world, each of us must more fundamentally achieve our own healing, which puts us in the strongest position to relieve the world of suffering.

2. The world resists salvation because it is immersed in fear, which considers love its enemy and seeks to get rid of it.

3. The world changes when we change our mind about the world. The first step to living in a new world is to see a new world.

4. Every person is vital to world healing. While this quest may seem unattainable or arrogant, it is the mission for which we were all born.

5. External healing comes naturally when we realize that what we seek to make whole is already whole. What is whole is invulnerable and can never be threatened.

6. Each of us has the strength and support to change the world. When we find the courage to accept our gifts and deliver them, genuine transformation happens.

Prayers, Affirmations, and Blessings

The Healer's Prayer

(From *A Course in Miracles* Text, Chapter 2)

This prayer is powerful and effective when used before you enter into any situation about which you feel anxious, such as treating a patient or client, preparing for an important meeting, or public speaking. It is soothing to the soul and creates miraculous results.

I am here only to be truly helpful.

I am here to represent Him Who sent me.

I do not have to worry about what to say or what to do, because He Who sent me will direct me.

I am content to be wherever He wishes, knowing He goes there with me.

I will be healed as I let Him teach me to heal.

Feel free to substitute "Higher Power," "Spirit," "She," "Love," or any other term that more comfortably represents God, rather than the masculine pronoun, if you wish.

I like to vary the last line to become, "I will be healed as I let Him heal through me."

Prayer for Physical Healing for Yourself

I now open to the pure and perfect power of God to manifest perfect healing and well-being in my body. The love and wisdom that created the entire universe guides all the cells and organs in my body to impeccably perform their intended function. I relax and allow my true nature of godly light to shine into full expression. There can be no disease in God. Because I am created in the image and likeness of a perfect God, there can be no disease in me. I now claim total wellness and I allow infinite energy, aliveness, ease, delight, and full function to express in my physical body and all of my activities.

Prayer for Emotional Healing

I trust that my life is unfolding in divine order. I do not need to worry about anything because I am God's beloved child, and God takes care of God's children. Everything I need is provided for me in the perfect way and timing. Fear is not of God, and therefore does not belong to me. Deep peace, confidence, and enthusiasm are my nature. I let go of attempting to control people and events, and I place all situations in the hands of God. My essence is love. All other emotions have nothing to do with me. I proceed calmly and joyfully, with an open, happy heart. My soul is at peace, and all is well.

Prayer for Healing of a Relationship

[Name of Person], I know that we share the same intention for love, harmony, and well-being. I recognize the goodness of your soul, and you recognize the goodness of mine. A joyful, peaceful, mutually supportive relationship is more important to me than any worldly matter. Our loving beings are in perfect communication, regardless of any appearances otherwise. My divine self speaks to your divine self. There is no discord in God, and there cannot be disharmony between us. I love and bless you, I want the best for you, and I know you want the best for me. I release our relationship to Higher Power, knowing that God uses all relationships for blessing, and a happy outcome is assured.

Prayer for Physical, Mental, Emotional, or Prosperity Healing of Another Person

[Name of Person], I see you as whole, perfect, successful, and divinely expressing. I rise beyond any illusion of illness or problem, and I claim wellness for you now. My vision of your best self calls you to rise and claim it for yourself and manifest it. You are a being of divine light, and that is the only truth about you. I see you functioning well in every dimension of your life. Your guides and angels are with you, delivering direction and healing as you need it. I see only perfection in you and around you. You are healed, whole, and empowered in the light of God's pure love.

Prayer for Prosperity

I live in a universe of total, utter prosperity. God created all of life in lavish supply for all of God's children. I am heir to the kingdom that provides all the good I need whenever

I need it. I recognize all thoughts of lack or emptiness as illusions, and I release them now. I claim my divine right to prosper in every way. I drop any anxious striving, I relax and clear the way for my good to find me in brilliant, miraculous ways. I do not dictate the avenue through which my sustenance comes; I leave all pathways of manifestation up to the Source of All Good. The universe is even extravagant, generating more than enough for everyone. I accept my worth to enjoy splendid riches for myself, overflowing to support others. I am honored to participate in divine circulation that keeps the universe functioning in opulent expression.

Prayer for Guidance

The God who created me guides me to my highest good at every moment. Divine wisdom is given to me in every situation I encounter. The mind of God is my mind; I know all that God knows. The Holy Spirit reaches into my life, illuminating my path. As I connect with my heart, I know what to do to create the best outcomes for myself and everyone I touch. I cease attempting to navigate my life with my intellect only, and I use the wisdom of my soul to access all the answers I need. I know everything I need to know to make the perfect choices before me. The God that guides me now guides me always in the perfect way and timing.

Prayer for Right Livelihood

There is a right and perfect path for the expression of my talent and passion. I claim that path for myself now, in co-creation with the Mind and Heart that seeded my vision deep within my soul. I do not have to settle for a livelihood that is in any way unfulfilling, out of integrity, or a mismatch to my true gifts. I have divinely inspired ideas and services to offer, and the universe provides the perfect means for me to express them. I deserve to be prospered and rewarded lavishly for the unique gifts I deliver to the world. I delight in using my talents and passions to help other people improve their lives. I now claim my right livelihood, and accept God's help to take care of all details.

Prayer for Success of a Project

I dedicate this project to Higher Power that it may serve all for whom it is intended. The Law of Attraction will join all the right people through this endeavor, enrich their lives, and return spiritual and material reward to me and all involved. I trust my guidance to participate in this project, and I know that the Mind that seeded this idea within me will deliver it with impeccable timing, relevance, and positive results for everyone it is intended to serve.

Prayer for Safe, Easy, Successful Travel

I set out on my journey with faith and positive vision, knowing that God goes with me and supports me wherever I am. The brilliant plan of synchronicity joins me with all the right people, events, and experiences to create delightful, successful travel. I am always safe and in the flow of wellness. I achieve my goals and return fulfilled, relaxed, and uplifted.

Prayer for World Well-Being

I behold the Planet Earth and all the people in all nations thriving. I hold the vision of life on Earth as God intended it. I surround the globe with healing light, replacing any appearances of lack, discord, or darkness. I see all cultures flourishing, true to their unique gifts and beauties, living in harmony with others. The peace of God fills the hearts of all people. I open to the experience of heaven on Earth, and I dedicate my life to uplift others wherever I go. I place the world and all its affairs in God's hands, and watch miracles unfold to enact God's will of love in the hearts and lives of all people everywhere, for all time. And so it is.

ACKNOWLEDGMENTS

It would be impossible to thank everyone who has contributed to my healing and well-being, and shown me how to support others in their healing process. Every spiritual teacher I have worked with, every mentor, every guru, every nonphysical guide, and many medical practitioners have served as lights and delivered kindness that has relieved my own pain and helped me help others to relieve theirs.

In particular, I wish to acknowledge the immaculate teachings of Jesus Christ, Hilda Charlton, Carla Gordan, Mary and the Guides, *A Course in Miracles,* Meher Baba, and Paramahansa Yogananda, who have all given me deep insights into how healing happens. I have also been inspired and uplifted by the model of healer Bruno Gröning, Abraham-Hicks, and Bashar.

More personally, I continue to acknowledge my beloved partner Dee Winn for her ongoing support of me and my work. Her love, energy, and well-considered ideas are a huge blessing to me personally and professionally.

I further appreciate Alyssa Freeland for her manuscript review and suggestions, as well as the medical practitioners I respect who have generously offered their support and testimonials:

Dr. Catherine O'Connell, Dr. Peter Nieman, Dr. Frances Delahanty, Dr. Teresa Reid, Dr. Michael Klaper, Dr. Matt Lyon, Dr. Deval Doshi, Corinne Zupko, Michele Stelling, and Heather Han.

Our cover designer Elena Karoumpali and interior designer Riann Bender have done a fabulous job. I am so grateful for their artistic skill and attunement to the themes of the book and the intention we share for readers to enjoy the best possible experience.

My respect and acknowledgment to all healers who devote themselves to relieve suffering, and to everyone who accepts their role in their own healing process, and is willing to receive well-being from the Source of All Life.

About the Author

Alan Cohen, M.A., holds degrees in psychology and human organizational development. He is the author of 30 popular inspirational books, including the best-selling *A Course in Miracles Made Easy* and the award-winning *A Deep Breath of Life*. He is a contributing writer for the #1 New York Times best-selling series *Chicken Soup for the Soul,* and he is featured in the book *101 Top Experts Who Help Us Improve Our Lives*. His books have been translated into 30 foreign languages. Alan has taught at Montclair State College, Omega Institute for Holistic Studies, and en*theos Academy for Optimal Living. He is a featured presenter in the award-winning documentary *Finding Joe,* celebrating the teachings of Joseph Campbell. His work has been presented on CNN and Oprah.com and in *USA Today, The Washington Post,* and *Huffington Post*. His monthly column *From the Heart* is published in magazines internationally. Alan is the founder and Director of the Foundation for Holistic Life Coaching. He presents programs on themes of life mastery, spiritual development, and vision psychology. For information on Alan Cohen's books, seminars, life coach training, videos and audio recordings, and online courses, visit: www.alancohen.com

Learn More
with Alan Cohen

If you have enjoyed and benefited from *The Master Keys of Healing*, you may want to deepen your understanding and inspiration by participating in Alan Cohen's in-person seminars, online courses, life coach training, or online subscription programs.

Inspirational Quote for the Day—An uplifting idea e-mailed to you each day (free)

Monthly e-Newsletter—Insightful articles and announcements of upcoming events (free)

The Coaching Room—A weekly online meeting during which Alan offers brief coaching (free)

Wisdom for Today—A stimulating life lesson e-mailed to you daily

Live Webinars—Interactive uplifting programs on topics relevant to spirituality, self-empowerment, and holistic living

Online Courses—In-depth experiential exploration of healing, relationships, prosperity, prayer, metaphysics, and time management

Life Coach Training—Become a certified professional holistic life coach or enhance your career and personal life with coaching skills

A Course in Miracles Retreat—A residential program to empower you to master the principles and skills of this life-changing course

For information about all of these programs,
new products and events, and more, visit

www.alancohen.com

Made in the USA
Las Vegas, NV
12 October 2022

57101745R00146